A LETTER TO MY DYING MOTHER

A LETTER TO MY DYING MOTHER

Surviving in the West

An Abridged Edition

Robert Peprah-Gyamfi

Perseverance Books

A Division of Thank You Jesus Books

Loughborough, Leicestershire, UK

A LETTER TO MY DYING MOTHER
Surviving in the West
An Abridged Edition

PERSEVERANCE BOOKS
A division of Thank You Jesus Books

For information, please contact:
Thank You Jesus Books
P.O.Box 8505
LOUGHBOROUGH
LE11 9BZ
UK

ISBN: 978-0-9570780-0-0

www.thankyoujesusbooks.com

To my father Opanin Kofi Gyamfi, whose decision to spend his last penny to ensure the best education for his children helped tap our talents.

CONTENTS

Acknowledgements

M y heartfelt thanks go to God Almighty, Creator of heaven and earth, for imparting the wisdom needed to write this book.

Rita, my wife, together with our children Karen, David, and Jonathan, also deserve my thanks and appreciation for their support and encouragement, which enabled me to persevere to the successful conclusion of this work.

I am also grateful to Dr Charles Muller of Diadembooks.com for carrying out the editorial work and for writing the preface.

Preface

This is an immensely entertaining and enlightening book, infused with humour and highlighted with moments of bittersweet poignancy. Robert has written the book as though it were a letter to his mother on her deathbed, telling her about how the way life in the West—in Germany, especially, where he now practises as a medical doctor—differs from the rural, traditional village life of Ghana where he grew up, a traditional African setting which is where his mother struggled to keep body and soul alive, going to the fields to do backbreaking work planting and reaping the meagre crops of cocoa and other foodstuffs, walking miles to fetch water for her home in a village where there was no running water or electricity, yet always managing to share what she had with her family and the less fortunate members of the village.

She was a woman who, dying at about the age of 75 (no one was certain of her exact age, since her birth was never recorded), knew no other life. What, indeed, would she have thought of the rushing trains and sleek cars in Germany, underground railways, the sophisticated and efficient hospitals, the supermarkets crammed with any amount of meat of all varieties, of crops, of canned food—you name it! In her village eating chicken was a luxury reserved only for Christmas day—and then only if there was enough to go round after she remembered all the less well-off members of her community!

When she was seriously ill, people had to find a lorry to flag down to take her to hospital, and the journey might have taken days! What would she have thought of emergency rescue helicopters in Germany, or of intensive care units where a person who might have been declared dead back home can be kept alive and even restored to full health!

The picture that emerges of Amma Owusuah, the old lady from Mpintimpi, is one of a very loveable and disarming personality committed to her belief in God. Robert tells me that she never learnt to read or write, and indeed was not able to converse in the "Queen's language", so had I met her, I would not have been able to sit down and chat about our diverse, and perhaps common, problems. But I would love to have had the opportunity of sitting with her, perhaps with some palm wine to hand, and had Robert to interpret for us, as we solved the problems of the world.

Charles Muller
Diadem Books
www.diadembooks.com

Introduction

A heartfelt desire that could not be realised.

I can't help wondering how mother would have reacted had she had the opportunity in her lifetime to visit Hanover in Germany, a city in the industrialised West.

Born into a little village, Amantia, located about 170 kilometres to the northwest of Accra in Ghana, West Africa, she later moved to settle in another village not far from the first. That was after she married father. Despite the fact that the second village bears the rather big name, Mpintimpi, it is about three times smaller than the first. It is in these two villages that mother spent almost all her days on earth.

Life in both villages reflects a true picture of rural life in a typical developing country. Among other things, the inhabitants have to do without such essential amenities as running water, electricity, or easy access to medical care and good and easily accessible roads. Apart from battery-operated transistor radios, the inhabitants in many such places have no or little access to some of the inventions of modern man—televisions, video-recorders, CD-players, refrigerators, washing machines, personal computers, etc.

At the other end of the spectrum is Hanover, a city located in a typical western industrialised country. There almost all the achievements of man at the end of the 20th century are on display.

Shortly after she emerged from the Hanover International Airport, I would have asked one of the numerous taxis queued up on the taxi ranks, the great majority of them latest models of Mercedes, to drive her to my apartment near the central part of the northern German city. The approximately ten-kilometre ride home would no doubt have fascinated her. She would surely have noticed the beautiful roads filled with cars of the best quality, the beautiful houses lining each side of the broad dual-carriage road, the beautiful light-green streetcars gliding to their destinations through the city to facilitate the rapid lifestyles of the city dwellers, not to mention the many gleaming brand-new cars parked in the yards of various car dealers waiting for their buyers. At home, in the living room of even an ordinary student she would have found furniture of quite good shape, a quite new colour TV as well as a video-recorder and a hi-fi system.

After she had rested for the day, I would on the next day have taken her on a sightseeing tour of the city. She would have had the first opportunity in her life to ride on the underground! Coming out at the central railway station, I would have taken her window-shopping through some of the several large department stores found there. How would she have reacted at the sight of the abundant stocks of goods of all kinds on display?

I would also have taken her to the Hanover Medical School. Of course, I would want to show her the place where I learnt my profession. Near the main entrance to the main building we would probably have seen the emergency helicopter parked in a nearby yard. The crew might be gathered in a little room in the vicinity, ready at any moment to fly to the aid of a seriously ill or injured person somewhere.

Inside the mighty building housing the various wards, she would, with all certainty, have been impressed by the very tidy and orderly environment. On a visit to a typical ward, she would have found the doctors, nurses and other hospital personnel briskly going about their duties in their unstinting efforts to bring health to their patients.

At the end of the day's excursion, mother, who was fond of talking and who was rarely short of words to express herself on any occasion, would, for the first time in her life, probably be at a loss to find adequate words to describe her experience. It would have dawned on her how different the world she was used to was to the one unfolding before her eyes. Sadly, mother departed this life on 5th July 1994, before my plans to invite her to visit me in Germany could materialise.

The idea of writing this book came to me the moment the news regarding her imminent death reached me in Germany, where I have lived a little over ten years. From the tone of my brother Kwame, known as Edmund, two years my senior, when he broke the news of mother's illness to me on the phone, I realised I would, with all certainty, not make it fast enough back home to be with the gravely ill old woman while she was still alive.

I therefore decided to despatch this long letter through a fictitious courier who, by chance, was flying to Ghana the next day, to let my dying mother know all that she would have seen, heard or experienced on a visit to this part of the world.

1

The kind gesture of a retired judge

Talaverastr. 2
30163 Hanover
Germany
1st July 1994

Dear Mother,

Word has just reached me that you are critically ill. This has come as a surprise to me since in the last letter I received from home—about three weeks ago—I was told everyone was quite well. I learnt of the sad news through a call Kwame made to me this afternoon. He had to travel a distance of about 170 kilometres to Accra, our capital, to make the call. According to him, you fell ill about three weeks ago. From what he told me I understand that, as is common practice in many parts of the country on such occasions, the family first used the resources of traditional medicine in seeking a cure. Instead of improving, your condition worsened rapidly.

Barely a week after the onset of the disease, you were no longer in a position to either eat or walk on your own. The family therefore decided to take you to hospital. Your bad state of health did not permit them to transport you by means of the usual wooden trucks that occasionally pass Amantia on their journey to the district capital, Akim Oda, where the next available hospital also happens to be located.

Fortunately a well-to-do individual, a retired magistrate judge in a large town, is said to have moved there recently to settle in the native village of his wife. According to Kwame, the well-to-do individual possesses a saloon car, something very unusual for an inhabitant of the rural areas of our country. This most recent inhabitant of the village, being aware of your critical condition, offered to drive you, at his own expense, to the hospital at Nkawkaw, well over 100 kilometres away.

Kwame went on to report that the two weeks you spent in hospital did not bring any significant improvement in your condition. Instead, your condition continued to deteriorate with every day. Finally a point came when everybody began to predict the worst. After consulting each other, the key members of the extended family who had travelled to the hospital to visit you decided to appeal to the doctors to allow them to take you home to spend your last days on earth in familiar surroundings.

Apart from enabling members of your large extended family as well as some of your numerous admirers in the village to keep vigil at your bedside to offer you solidarity in your battle with death, it would also prevent the situation that would lead to your body being deposited in the hospital mortuary for a while prior to the final transport home.

You had explicitly asked us to prevent a situation like that. After all, you had often asked why the body of a person who in life hated anything that was frozen should be made to freeze after she has departed this life!

As Kwame was leaving the hospital for Accra to make the call, preparations were underway to take you back to Amantia. Barring the unforeseeable happening, you would end your earthy journey in the same little village where it began about 75 years ago.

As you might expect, I am very saddened about the news of your imminent departure. It is not the fact of your passing away as such that is the main source of my sorrow. As a matter of fact, we need to be grateful to God for His protection that enabled you to attain your age. It is no secret that mainly as a result of the harsh living conditions prevailing in our part of the world many an individual only dreams of reaching the age you were privileged to see. Still, I have at least three reasons to be disappointed at the thought of your approaching death.

In the first place, I had been making plans to invite you to visit me here to see things for yourself before you depart this life.

Secondly, it has always been my desire to stand by your deathbed to bid a personal farewell before you say adieu to our world of many faces.

Above all, I'm disappointed that you did not live to enjoy the fruits of your hard labour. Indeed, after all the hardships you had to endure in the face of abject poverty, disease and want, to raise up your eight children, one might have expected you to be the recipient of a degree of pampering in your old age.

Much as we would have wished for that, financial constraints prevented us from going to the extent we would have wanted. Just at the time when a couple of us are gradually beginning to see some light at the end of the dark tunnel of life that we have been treading for some years, you have to depart us! As the saying goes, however, man proposes, but God disposes.

I am making plans to come home as soon as possible. I guess you have some idea as to the great distance between me and home. One cannot just take one's bag and baggage to the airport and catch the next flight home; instead, one has first to make reservations with an airline. From my information, the earliest I can catch the next flight to Ghana is in about two weeks' time.

Fortunately, I've just learnt that a Ghanaian friend living a couple of streets away from me is flying to Ghana tomorrow. By sheer coincidence he happens to be a native of Muronaamu, the little settlement about five kilometres to the north of Amantia. I've decided to take advantage of the unique opportunity to send, through him, what is likely to be my last communication with you.

In my letter I will attempt to give you a detailed account of life in this part of the world—the part of the world we refer to at home as *Aburokyire*. That way, if even in a faint manner, an attempt will have been made on my part to satisfy one of the great desires of your life—an opportunity, if even for once, to get a glimpse of the area of the globe that arouses various fantasies in the minds of many at home.

The society here where I live has, indeed, achieved a very high standard of living In any given town or city one visits, one may, for example, come across several supermarkets fully stocked with goods of all kind. The goods are not on display only to be looked at; the average citizens, for their part, have in general enough purchasing power at their disposal to afford the basic necessities of life.

An environment abounding in material goods of all kind has given rise to a population that is inclined, accordingly, towards acquiring as much of the material things available as possible. The unceasing drive of the individual to satisfy his or her material needs can lead such a person to neglect other important issues of life, however. That's the observation I've made since being here. Yes, indeed, the quest for material satisfaction has led many a person in this affluent society to neglect, either partially or entirely, the spiritual realm of human existence.

Possession of wealth, which enables the individual to meet all, or almost all material needs, makes the concept of a power who cares, and who one may pray to for help in times of need, unattractive to many. Indeed, the almost universal belief in God that prevails in our part of the world is missing here.

Furthermore, due to the fact that most people have control over sufficient material goods to be independent, the need to approach their neighbours to ask for anything seldom arises. This has contributed on its part to the individualisation of society. Consequently many people live isolated lives here. Bonds between people, even close relatives, might as well be described as superficial at best. Most people seem to be concerned with their own selves. As someone put it, the society here has become based on the concept of "each one for himself or herself and God for us all".

Life here is, without any doubt, more comfortable than that found at your end. Whether the residents here are more satisfied with their life compared with the inhabitants living under the harsh conditions prevailing at home is an issue that remains debateable. Having said this by way of introduction, I will venture to tackle the formidable task I have set myself.

2

The concept of Aburokyire

❧

To begin with, I want to talk about the term *Aburokyire* as applied at home. Generally, the term is used to refer to foreign lands. This could lead to misunderstanding in the minds of many, however.

Broadly speaking, a country like Nigeria or Togo or Uganda, could, from the point of view of someone in Ghana, be regarded as Aburokyire. It is no secret, however, that hardly anyone who speaks of Aburokyire at home ever has any of the countries mentioned above in mind. Instead, Aburokyire has become synonymous with the countries of the western industrialised world. For someone like you, Aburokyire stands for the dwelling place of the white man, who is generally regarded from our perspective as being extremely wealthy.

Few people of your age and level of knowledge about things of this world are aware that Aburokyire, even in the strict sense of its meaning, is made up of several countries. That brings to my mind the experience I had during one of my stays at home.

Whilst I was visiting Amantia, an elderly woman approached me with a piece of paper in her hand. It contained the address of someone (it turned out to be her son) living in one of the countries of Aburokyire known as the United States of America. The elderly resident requested me to visit her son and extend her greetings on my return. What she was not aware of was the fact that Germany where I resided was an entirely different country from the US. Not only are the two countries several thousand kilometres apart, the two are also separated, among others, by a huge mass of water, known as the Atlantic Ocean.

Indeed, Aburokyire, just as in the case of Abibiman, or Africa, does not consist of a single country but of several different nations. Apart from the two countries I have just referred to, other countries of Aburokyire include England (Enyiresi-Aburokyire), France (Frenkye Aburokyire), Portugal (Portugiisi Aburokyie), and so forth.

In the minds of many people at home, the term Aburokyire could as well be interchanged with terms like "great wealth", "paradise on earth", "luxury" and "enjoyment without end", etc. This thinking, in my opinion, has helped to engrave various illogical presumptions, conclusions, inferences, etc., in the minds of many individuals at home.

I have in the meantime come to realise that what I have just said is true not only of citizens of Ghana but also of those living in several areas of the developing world. The reason why this is so, is something we could better leave for the experts in such matters.

If only matters would end there! But no! The false assumption referred to has given rise to further false associations, presumptions, generalisations and so on. One such presumption, in my opinion, has come about because there has been an inclination, false as it is, to import a "mathematical" supposition—because country A is very wealthy, Mr or Mrs Z living there must be very wealthy as well—into the discussion. Drawing that conclusion is not only misleading—it is also potentially dangerous. Let's even assume that 99.9% of residents of Country A are indeed wealthy. That could still mean that 0.1% of them have to struggle hard to make ends meet.

There is no question that the countries under consideration are far richer than, for example, a country such as Ghana. The average citizen here is also far wealthier than his or her counterpart in Ghana. It is still true to say that there are a considerable number of natives here who also have to struggle to make ends meet. Their situation could be even more frustrating: in a society where the great majority are poor, one tends to console oneself with the thought that he or she is not alone in the boiling pot. Not so in a situation when circumstances force one to go by foot in an environment where the majority are riding on bikes!

Unfortunately, many a person at home sees in Aburokyire a kind of paradise on earth, a place where money literally floats on the street! This picture of the western world as a world that abounds in wealth is, unfortunately, so much entrenched in the minds of so many at home that it is difficult to imagine that it could ever be eradicated.

I must admit, however, that prior to my arrival here, I also nurtured that illusion of abundant wealth about life here. Does this attitude have something to do with our colonial past? I think the question does not entirely miss the target! I recall the time when I was growing up at Mpintimpi. On those rare occasions when the vehicle of a person of European descent happened to pass by or even stop in the village to purchase some foodstuff, all the children in the village—including myself—rushed out of our homes and ran after the passing vehicle or surrounded the European who had stopped in the village, and began to cry on top of our voices: "*Oburoni koko, kye me kapere; oburoni koko kye me kapere!*" (White person, please give me a penny; white person, please give me a penny!)

This idea of the poor Africans beseeching the wealthy and generous European to shower presents on them has not, I suspect, completely deserted some of us. Some have coined the term "beggar-mentality" in regard to the African to describe this curious attitude.

A new aspect of our tendency to look to others for solutions to our problems emerged after citizens from our country began to arrive here. All of a sudden people at home came to regard their relatives and friends as well-to-do's who were in the position to provide for all their monetary and material needs—thinking, perhaps, that there exists in Aburokyire a magnetic force that helps to draw abundant hard currency into the pockets of whoever lives there; or perhaps that money rains down on residents from the skies, a kind of manna, one might say: they expect their relatives and friends here to grow rich overnight.

It is in the light of what I have just said that you might perhaps come to terms with what I am about to narrate. Not long ago a student arrived here from Ghana on an exchange programme that was to last for about four months. The scholarship attached to the programme was just enough to cover his boarding and lodging. In the end he hardly had money left for anything else. Barely two weeks after his arrival here the first letter reached him from home. It came from his father:

Dear son,

Greetings from your father. Immediately after your departure I was suddenly taken ill. I need to be sent to hospital for treatment. Unfortunately, no one in the family is in a position to bring up the needed money. You would do well to come to my aid immediately—or you will not see me alive again. The rest of the family extend their greetings.

I am your father.

A second letter followed on the heels of the first. This time it was the turn of one of his nieces:

Dear uncle,

I need to acquire some textbooks. They are very expensive to buy here. [The letter went on to list the books in question.]

I will be grateful if you could buy them for me when you return to Ghana.

It is me, your niece.

The third letter to arrive within the first two weeks of his stay in Germany came from his best friend. He wrote to express his thanks to the Almighty for the safe arrival of his best friend on the soil of Europe. After dwelling a while on issues of general interest he went on to "business"—*Please be so kind as to buy me a camera and a walkman when you return to Ghana!*

3

The return of "Star Black"

It is an open secret that many of our nationals, especially among the young adults, yearn for the opportunity to settle in this part of the world. What many at home are not aware of is that there are strict immigration laws in this country to prevent outsiders from settling here.

I must confess that prior to my arrival here, I also had no ideas in that regard. As far as Germany was concerned, I had only heard from others that a foreigner could be granted leave to stay there after applying for political asylum.

That at the end of the day, the prospect of an asylum seeker from Ghana ever being recognised as a political refugee, a status that would entitle that individual to proper residence and working permits was something that was not known to me. I will return to the issue of political asylum , called "Aduro", by the Ghanaian community here, later in my deliberations.

Yes indeed there are very stringent visa and immigration laws prevailing in several countries of the western industrialised world, to prevent outsiders from settling there. Being , as it were, a developed enclave in a world where the overwhelming majority struggle daily to survive, countries in the rich industrialised world, go to great extends to prevent their countries being flooded by what they term economic refugees. By the term economic refugees they mean people who come here in search of greener pastures. Whether they are wholly right in their assertion that almost everyone from the developing world seeking to settle in their countries does so for economic reasons is open to debate, a debate I do not want to engage you in at this stage of your life.

As I just mentioned , there are restrictive immigration and visa regulations in place in Germany and elsewhere in the West. If, for example, I had invited you to visit me here, you could not just have picked up your bag, made it to Accra International Airport and boarded the next flight bound for Germany.

No, you would first have had to apply to the Passport Authority in Accra for a passport. You would then have presented the passport and other supporting documents at the German Embassy in Accra and have applied for a visa.

The most important supporting document would have been money. Yes you would have had to produce sufficient evidence to convince them that you or your big-headed son in their country inviting you, had sufficient funds to support you during your stay in their country.

Also of equal importance: the embassy staff would have questioned you extensively to convince themselves that you would be willing to leave their country and return to your deprived little village on expiry of your visa. In view of your age, they would probably not have attached much weight to that aspect of the interview. They would have probably assumed that a person of your age might not want to overstay her visa. Even if you wanted to, they probably would have reasoned, the onset of the winter with the accompanying freezing temperatures would likely compel an elderly woman who throughout her life was not used to anything apart from the scorching African heat to pack bag and baggage and rush to catch the next flight back into the tropical sun.

The situation would have been completely different if I had invited any of your three daughters, Adwoa Donkor, Adwoa Manu or Afia Serwah, none of whom is over 30. Indeed I have my strong doubts that in their case, the embassy would ever have issued visas, even if they satisfied all the requirements. The visa authorities might have reasoned that they would follow the example of many of their age from the developing world who entered here with tourists visas and went underground on expiry of their stay permit instead of leaving for their respective countries.

You may want to know how, despite all I have said in regard to the immigration laws persisting here, some of our citizens have managed to settle here. Well the saying has it that charity begins at home, so I will use my own case as an example as I attempt to answer your question.

When I attended Oda Secondary School at Akim Oda, our district capital, my best friend was George Kwadwo Awuah Yeboah, known by us as George for short. He lived with his uncle at Akim Oda, but like every student attending the second cycle institution, was a boarding student.

In due course George informed me that one of his cousins, Kwasi Boakye, popularly known by his alias name, "Star Black", was resident in Germany. One afternoon, my friend came to me, a lot of excitement written in his face, and began.

"Kwasi is on a short visit from Germany! I am going home at the weekend to meet him!"

"May I come with you?" I inquired.

"Of course you can!"

So we obtained permission from our housemaster and left school the following Saturday for a short visit to Kwadwo's home.

The visitor from Germany looked really splendid, mother! Not only did he look well-fed, the clothes he wore were also imposing and magnificent. Besides showing us several wonderful items he had brought along, he also showed us pictures he had taken in Aburokyire. The conclusion I drew from that encounter was that life in Aburokyire might indeed be luxurious.

In due course, I came across several other Ghanaians who had returned from Germany and other western countries. The *Burgers*, the term we use for our nationals resident in the West on a visit home, all seemed to be doing very well. I learnt that many of the *Burgers* had sought for political asylum whilst in the West. In the case of Germany, I was told that the right of an individual to seek political asylum in that country was enshrined in the constitution.

"The moment the words *political asylum* ensued from the lips of a stranger who had just arrived in that country at the immigration check point, that individual was entitled to a state permit, accommodation and welfare benefits!" some of the rumours went on to claim.

Despite such claims, I personally I did not entertain the thoughts of ever travelling outside the country, not even to one of Ghana's direct neighbours. How could the son of an impoverished woman like yourself and Agya Kofi Gyamfi ever harbour such ideas?

The idea to travel to Europe first came to me when I failed in my bid to gain admission to medical school in Ghana. Mainly as a result of the suffering and hardships prevailing at Mpintimpi and the surrounding areas, I wanted to become a doctor to help in my own small way to alleviate the situation.

Eventually, I got to know that tuition was free in all German universities, foreign students included.

If only I could make it to Germany, I could eventually make it to medical school, I said to myself. How could I do so without the financial means to purchase even a plane ticket? In the end I joined a friend of mine who was on his way to Nigeria to work to purchase a ticket for the US to study there. Like my friend my aim was also to work to earn my plane ticket for Germany.

Initially, I had to do bone-breaking jobs at construction sites in Lagos to survive in Nigeria. After staying there for about two years, I earned enough money to enable me to purchase a ticket for a flight to Germany. As I embarked on my adventure into the unknown, I had no idea what to expect.

On our arrival in East Berlin, a pleasant surprise awaited me and a group of other Ghanaians on the flight. Shortly after coming out of the airport buildiing, we bumped into a group of Africans on the street. As it turned out, they happened to be from Ghana. Happily, they invited us to their place of residence. They made it known to us that the only way we could avoid being deported back to Ghana was to apply for political asylum. In the end, I saw no alternative but to apply for political asylum.

4

The three friends credited with the discovery of political asylum

he matter of political asylum! There are so many wild stories and rumours circulating among the Ghanaian population here, surrounding the asylum process, I could end up writing volumes should I decide to dwell on even a small fraction of them.

How then did our countrymen and women get to know that one could apply for political asylum in Germany?

I want to narrate one of the wild stories circulating among the Ghanaian population here to that effect. Though unsubstantiated, it is still regarded as being credible by many of those who hold on to it.

Here it goes:

Several years ago, at the time when citizens of our newly-independent country began to travel to Germany, they could enter the country and stay for three months without a visa. All that the traveller from Ghana needed was a passport, a round-ticket, and enough hard currency to show at the immigration check. After the expiry of that period one was required to either leave the country or regularise his or her stay by other means.

After tasting the comfortable living conditions here, many of the new arrivals refused to return home. Instead they chose to stay on illegally. Three friends from Ghana decided to do the same at the expiry of their three- month stay.

In time all of the three found employment as factory hands in different companies. They left their residence early each day for work. After work each of them hurried home. None was at ease on reaching home until all the others returned safely.

For several months things worked in their favour. A day came, however, when two of them returned home from work to find their friend, usually the first to do so, had not yet arrived! Nervousness descended on them. Where on earth had their companion, known for his reliability and punctuality, gone? The hours passed by; nothing happened.

The two friends spent much of the night praying and hoping for the return of their friend—but he failed to turn up. The days turned into weeks with still no signs of his whereabouts. Although very desperate and worried, there was little they could do other than wait and pray. Illegal immigrants that they were, they did not have the courage to approach the police to notify them about their missing compatriot for fear they would be arrested and placed on the next flight back home.

Their suspicion was that their friend had perhaps fallen into the hands of the immigration authorities who probably had deported him. But if that were the case, why had he not written from Ghana? Or was he still being detained in Germany? If so, why had he failed to give them even a single call to help alleviate their fears? Hope began to give way to despair as a month passed and still nothing reached them concerning the plight or whereabouts of their friend.

One evening, just as they were pondering their next move, their doorbell rang. Who could it be at that hour of the day? Had the police found their address on their friend? Tension began to mount. The bell sounded the second and then the third time.

"Who is there?" they inquired simultaneously.

"Do not be afraid, boys!" the microphone beamed the voice of their friend into the room! "It is I, the "prodigal son"!"

"Incredible!" both shouted on the top of their voices.

With tears of joy they opened the door to welcome their friend home.

"Where have you been all this time?" they inquired as if with a single voice as soon as he entered.

"Friends, give me something to drink first! I have good news for you!"

"Tell us where you were and do not keep us any longer in suspense!" they persisted as one of them made for the refrigerator to find him something to drink.

"Take it from me, friends," he began at last, "there are indeed several good laws in this country!"

"What do you mean?"

"Yes indeed, this country has very good laws!" he repeated.

"Come on, tell us what you mean by that!"

At that stage the newcomer began his story.

"On the day in question I was busy doing my usual chores at my workplace when three officers arrived to check the work permits of the staff. I was the only one who failed to produce the required document. I was subsequently arrested and taken to the police station. After intensive interrogation they decided to deport me back to Ghana. They told me they would detain me until the necessary arrangement had been completed.

"One day a solicitor who had come to the prison to visit his client came across me. In the process the legal expert engaged me in a conversation. In the end he got to know why I was there.

"'Do not be scared, ' he comforted me. 'I will help you out of here.'

"'What do you mean?' I inquired, hardly able to believe my ears.

"'Wait a moment,' he replied and handed me a piece of paper. 'I assume you are informed about the current political situation in your home country?' he continued.

"'Of course I am,' I replied.

"'Good. Then sit down and formulate a statement indicating you belong to the opposition, and that you used to be a strong critic of the ruling military regime. You even went to the extent of organising a demonstration to protest against the policies of the military junta. As a result of your activities directed at the ruling government you were arrested and sent to a military detention camp. You met no less than a hundred other detainees there. They told you about the permanent torture they were subjected to.

"'Soon you also came to experience torture at first hand as you received beatings, electric shocks as well as other forms of humiliation. There was even talk of you being executed one day. You had cause to take those threats to your life seriously, for almost every day an inmate was whisked away by the military never to return again.

"'Fortunately one of the officers overseeing you happened to be your former schoolmate! With his assistance you managed to escape from detention. That was not the end; he also lent you enough money to facilitate your flight out of the country!'

"Armed with that statement the solicitor promised to file an application for political asylum on my behalf.

"A few days after that meeting, an immigrations officer called on me in prison to demand certain clarifications on my statement. To the question, why I had not forwarded my application immediately after my arrival in the country, or latest after my arrest, I could only reply that I did not know whom to contact on the matter.

"Shortly after that meeting, they decided to release me. I was given an address of a hotel where I would live free of charge. Besides that, I was given a ticket for a free ride on public transport as well as pocket money. I was assured of financial support so long as my application for political asylum had not been decided on.

"So, friends, I am free at last! I do not have to worry about how to pay for my accommodation, how to feed myself, how to receive medical care and things like that. So be quick and get your statements ready! I will direct you to the lawyer. You have to go there alone, however—I do not want him to get the impression I directed you there."

You can guess, mother, how the two friends reacted to his story! They immediately got to work writing their statements. After they had celebrated through much of the night the two presented their applications to the lawyer early the next morning. Eventually all three had their applications granted; from then on they began to enjoy the privileges due to them as political refugees.

This, according to the story, was how we got to know that someone running from persecution, mainly on political and religious grounds, could seek asylum in this country.

News has the tendency to spread like wildfire. Soon hundreds of citizens from our country had submitted their applications for political asylum.

Initially the authorities seemed to believe what the applicants had to say. As time went by and their number began to soar, suspicion began to arise. Not only could the stories formulated by some applicants be described as childish at best, but some applicants, when called for interviews, made statements that totally contradicted the earlier statements they had submitted at the time of their applications.

Ultimately measures were put in place with the aim of making the status of an asylum seeker as unattractive as possible. Initially the time that elapsed between application submission and decision making was quite considerable. Even in the case of a negative decision, the applicant was given the right of appeal to the courts. That could also help them gain time. By the time the final decision was made to ask a rejected applicant to leave the country, the applicant had either saved enough money to be ready to leave anyway in order to begin a business at home, or had been able to regularise his or her stay through other means.

Several years have passed since the first Ghanaian sought political asylum here. Over time the number of applicants, not only from Ghana but also from other countries in the developing world, has increased considerably. With that has come an increase in the social and political pressure for measures to be adopted to curb the influx.

As a result, the asylum laws in several countries in Aburokyire have been tightened, and tightened yet again, to the extent that if one were to compare the system to a fishing net stretched out along the path of a stream to prevent fish from entering a forbidden area, it could be described as capable of keeping even the smallest minnow in check! At the time of writing it is practically impossible for an applicant from a country like Ghana to have the slightest chance of success.

5

The student reluctant to call it quits

As I mentioned earlier on, my main aim of coming here was to study. Fortunately, after initial difficulty, I was admitted to the Hanover Medical School. With that, I was issued with a student's visa. It was usually issued on an annual basis. As long as I was a registered student, it was renewed without any difficulty.

That leads me to the other avenues by which a foreign citizen could be granted leave to stay in this country, if even for a limited period of time. As my example demonstrates, one of them is by way of a student's visa. The stay permit is usually revoked on completion of the course of study. One is then required to leave the country. Not a few students, especially from a developing country such as Ghana, when they are nearing the end of their studies resort to delay tactics to prolong their studies and so their stay.

An acquaintance of mine who happens to hail from Ghana, to avoid being asked to return to Ghana, studied so many different subjects that he ended up gaining the nickname "Professor" or "Prof" for short. (For your information, a professor is someone who has attained a high level in a particular field of study). His strategy was to register for another course of study just about the time a particular one was ending. As I mentioned earlier on, tuition is free for all at German universities, a fact that favoured his strategy.

In time, the immigration authorities became aware of the tricks of the *ewige Studenten* (professional students) and sought means to counter them. At the moment foreign students here usually regularly have to provide convincing proof of academic progress in their fields of study before their visas can be extended. After the expiry of a stipulated period of time, during which one is generally expected to have completed the field of study concerned, one risks having one's application for an extension of visa rejected.

6

Marriages convenient and inconvenient

I f one is neither a political refugee nor a student, another reason a foreigner from a country like Ghana may obtain permission to reside here is by way of marriage to a citizen of the country—or some other country that may be relevant. Formerly, only marriages to German citizens were recognised. Several years ago Germany became a member of the European Economic Community. At the time of writing, this privilege has been extended to marriages with citizens of other member countries of the community who have residential status here as well.

After such a marriage has lasted for a period of time, the foreigner may be granted permanent stay in the country of the spouse. Those willing to do so could even apply for citizenship of the countries of their spouses.

Time will not permit me to go into details on the issue of marriage of convenience. Indeed a lot of rumours are making their rounds to the effect that some foreign citizens wanting to stay on in the country, pay money to the natives to get them to marry them. Such marriages are not marriages in the real sense of the word as you and I understand them. Although the authorities are not unaware of such practices, it is not always easy for them to prove that the marriage is not genuine.

7

Letters from the underground

❦

Others, after all their attempts to legalise their stay have failed, just decide to stay on illegally. Such a step is not without risks, however. For one thing, one has to live with the constant fear of being arrested at any moment and being deported.

Illness or bad health might also bring the person living underground into difficulty. In Germany there exists a health insurance system that usually covers only citizens and the legal foreign residents. In case of illness, illegal residents who can afford it, can consult a family doctor. Matters can become complicated, however, if the affected person requires hospitalisation.

The cost of treatment in hospital in a country like Germany can be expensive. The hospital authorities could also notify the police, should it turn out that the patient is not in a position to pay.

This brings to mind the case that came to my notice when I worked occasionally as a court interpreter for the Twi language. It involved a Ghanaian lady. Several months before our meeting, she had married a German tourist she met at the Labadi Beach in Accra.

The German citizen had to return home shortly after the exchange of the marriage vows before a family judge at a registry in Accra. He left his newly-wedded spouse behind to apply for a visa at the German embassy in Accra.

The authorities, probably suspicious that it could be an example of a marriage of convenience, began to play delaying tactics on her application. Days turned into weeks to end up in months, yet there was no sign of the embassy issuing her a visa anytime soon.

Just about that time, the woman in question was diagnosed with a disease that the doctors in Ghana, for technical reasons, could not handle locally. When it came to their notice that her husband happened to be a German, they urged her to seek medical help in that country to avert the worst.

At that point, the newly-wed began to seek alternative means of joining her husband, instead of waiting for an official entry permit.

At last, she succeeded in making it to Germany on some else's passport. From the airport she boarded a train to Hanover where her husband was resident. Shortly after alighting from the train at the Hanover Central Station, she fainted, from internal bleeding, as she was later told. Soon an ambulance was speeding to her rescue. Finally she was admitted to hospital where she underwent emergency surgery. Happily she made a good recovery.

A week after her admission, she had recovered sufficiently to be interviewed in matters concerning her hospital bills. As a first step, the hospital authorities requested details of her health insurance.

"What do you mean by that?" she replied, bewildered, speaking through an interpreter. Soon the hospital administration realised she had neither a health insurance cover nor the funds to foot her bills herself. In the end they handed the case over to the police.

In the course of the investigation, her marital status became known to the authorities. Since she was married to a German national she could not be deported.

What about the hospital bills? That issue indeed was the subject of the court proceeding. In the end the bulk of the amount involved was taken care of by the insurance of her German husband. She was made to shoulder only a small proportion. Even as far as her part was concerned, the need for her to meet her obligation was suspended till she was deemed financially in a position to do so.

With some degree of luck, however, one could survive underground for a considerable time without being caught. One needs to abide by some unwritten rules and regulations, nevertheless. As far as possible, the person involved has to avoid visiting places where trouble could crop up, which in turn could cause the police to come round to restore order. Usually the first thing the law-enforcing agents do on their arrival is to check the identities of those in the immediate surroundings.

Besides that, one always has to possess a valid ticket for a ride on public transport, and avoid organising or attending loud parties—any situations that could lead neighbours to call the police to the scene, who in turn could check the identities of those around.

I shall end this chapter with a story I heard the other day about someone else's experience underground. The story has it that a countryman without proper residence papers decided to keep on him the passport of his sister who was a legal resident. His sister, who had resided in Aburokyire for several years, was content to carry a photocopy of her residence permit. Being very much at home with the local language, she knew how to defend herself should the police stop her to carry out an identity check.

The picture in the passport showed a person with a short haircut. According to the story, it was not easy for the beholder to determine the sex of the person by looking at it. The name of the holder might of course be expected to shed more light on the issue. You and I know, for example, that the Twi names such as "Akosuah Gyamfuah", "Yaa Serwaah", "Akua Nyamekye", are conferred only on the female person. During the early stages when we arrived here, at a time when the incident I am narrating was purported to have happened, not so many police officers here were so informed.

The story goes on to say that the brother was actually stopped on the street one day by two policemen! "Sir, we are from the CID. We are investigating a crime that happened in the neighbourhood. Could you please show us something to identify yourself?"

The man thought to himself: *This is the end of me!* Although he had reckoned with something like that, he had hoped and prayed that his fears would never be realised. There was no time to waste, however. Reaching into the pocket of his jacket, he removed the passport and handed it to them. His heart began to quicken. For the moment he pictured in his mind's eye a flight bound for Ghana with himself a passenger.

The officers first took a look at the picture in the passport, then back at him, then a further look at the picture. Next, they took a quick glance through the document. Finally they handed it back to him.

"Is everything okay?" the African inquired, hardly able to control his emotions.

"Yes, sir. We apologise for any inconveniences caused!"

"I am not offended!"

"Have a nice day, friend!"

"Same to you, sirs!"

He headed straight home. For the next few days he was too scared to go out.

8

German-Buroni

∞

In this chapter, I will attempt to give you a brief picture of what I have observed about residents of this country. As I mentioned above, Aburokyire, even in terms of the strictest definition, is made up of several countries.

Although a lot of what I will write about in this letter is generally true for most of the Aburokyire societies, there are some qualities that set some of the societies apart. However, I don't want to go into details or dwell on the qualities that, for example, differentiate Enyiresi-Aburokyire (England) from French-Aburokyire (France) or America-Aburokyire (USA) from Portugiisi Aburokyire (Portugal) etc.

As the saying goes, however, charity begins at home. As you are aware, I have all these years been living in German-Aburokyire (Germany). I have therefore considered it appropriate to dedicate a chapter to dwell briefly on some of the qualities that, in the opinion of many, singles out the Germans from many nationalities in the western world.

To make my task somewhat easier, I want to draw your attention to Papa Kwabena, the elderly distant relative of ours who lived at Mpintimpi all his life and who passed away a couple of years ago. You may recall the alias everyone in the village used to describe him. Indeed, almost everyone in the village used to call him "German-Buroni" which, translated, stands literally for "the white man from Germany."

Papa Kwabena, I am certain, will long be remembered in the village, both by friend and foe, for some of the qualities that singled him out from other members of our little community.

"German-Buroni!"—he was an orderly, disciplined and hard-working individual who had little patience for the non-hardworking and indolent. It does not end there. One could also describe him as a no-nonsense type of person who, for the most part, was not only serious with himself but also with the rest of the world around him. He had no patience with individuals who in his eyes were lazy. Neither could he condone nor tolerate anyone, be it a relative close or distant, friend or stranger, who in his opinion was not prepared to shed enough sweat to accomplish something in life. In that vein he was often at loggerheads with one of his own sons who appeared to him to be nothing else but a pack of idle bones.

It was Papa Kwabena's custom to leave home early in the morning to work on his farm. In the afternoon, one might see him returning from the fields with a heavy load made up of all possible items on his head as well as on both shoulders.

One would be mistaken, then, to suppose that the daily chores of German-Buroni had ended! No! After he had rested for a while, he got up once more, took his machete and headed for the woods yet again! One could only wonder what was driving him to the woods at that time of day. Was he on his way to inspect the traps he had set for rodents such as the grasscutter? Was he on his way to the Nwi River to inspect his fish traps? Was he on his way to get some assignment done on another field?

Two or three hours later one would find him returning to the village, once again bearing a heavy load. Even then it would be premature to conclude that the daily chores of "German-Buroni" beyond the borders of his home were over for the day. No! Minutes later he would be seen heading for the woods for the third time—God only knew what for!

Even during the later part of his life as his eyesight began to fail him, German-Buroni kept a firm hold of his principles. Although he could no longer visit his farms as often as he would want to, the necessary strength to enable him to come out to drive away offending children from his premises never forsook him.

I can only wonder how the inhabitants of our village came to liken the qualities of Papa Kwabena to that of the Germans, for they were indeed right in their judgement, for without doubt the qualities Papa Kwabena was endowed with reflect almost exactly those displayed by the average citizens of my host country.

Let us consider, for example, his attitude to work. The typical German seems similarly to be obsessed with work. Although the average co-inhabitant of German-Buroni at Mpintimpi could not altogether be described as lazy, it was Papa Kwabena's near-obsession with work that singled him out from the rest of the community. In the same manner, the attitude of the average citizen of this country towards work seems to single him or her out from many an inhabitant in other countries in Aburokyire.

If you ever made it to this country the two local items of vocabulary that would first stick in your memory would probably be *arbeit* as well as its cousin, *arbeitslos*. These two words are repeated several times daily—be it on radio, on TV, or in conversation between individuals. One might also come across them several times in the newspapers. What do they mean? *Arbeit* means work, a job, or, in the broad sense, employment. *Arbeitslos* is the opposite of the former and stands literally for no work, joblessness or unemployment.

At the beginning of every month, figures are issued showing how many new *arbeit* have been created the previous month and how many *arbeitslos* were able as a result to secure *arbeit*. At the end of the day, the balance is drawn to show how many people still remain *arbeitslos* despite the creation of several new *arbeit*.

The reading of the figures is followed by a short speech by the Director of the Department of Employment who tries to explain to the *arbeitslos* why the situation is as it is and to urge them to stand firm in the face of the difficulties they may be facing by dint of their being *arbeitslos*.

That part of the TV news may be followed by a piece showing an angry demonstration of people who may either be calling for an increase in salary or drawing attention to an impending threat of worker lay-offs in their company.

The Germans are dutiful and law-abiding people. There are traffic lights that regulate traffic in many towns and cities in several countries in the world. Pedestrians have special places where they may cross the road. At such points special traffic lights have been installed to regulate the times when people can cross. One has to stop at the red sign and walk at the green. In many countries, pedestrians do not take the regulation seriously. Many may wait for the green light only when the streets are busy with traffic; otherwise they may cross, even when the lights require them to wait. Visitors to Germany usually wonder how law-abiding the citizens here are. Even at midnight when few vehicles are seen on the roads, many a citizen here would tend to wait patiently for the sign to cross before doing so.

Residents here also have a craving for cleanliness and orderliness. In homes, in offices, in hospitals, etc., great pains are taken to ensure things are clean and tidy, or orderly. Some of my acquaintances from Ghana who clean private homes for their living, tell me when they arrive in some homes where they have been hired to tidy up, they begin to ask themselves why their owners decided to hire them to work there in the first place, for in the eyes of the worker in question the home was already perfectly clean!

It is rare to find Germans throwing or dumping litter on the streets. At short distances along the streets, dustbins have been placed where litter can be disposed of. What litter that eventually falls on the streets is regularly cleared away by workers specially employed for that purpose.

Orderliness extends to almost every sphere of life here. A Ghanaian friend of mine who has lived here for a considerable time once remarked, "Boy, I have lived here for years but I have yet to come across a lost banknote on the street!" No wonder, for almost everybody here possesses a wallet—or handbag—in which he or she keeps his or her money. The wallet may go missing together with the enclosed money, but not the money on its own.

Like German-Buroni, the residents here are serious-looking and very disciplined. One has to be careful not to be too noisy at certain times of the day, otherwise one risks the anger of his or her neighbour, who may even go to the extent of calling the police.

On the—streets this is particularly true of large towns and cities— everyone walks briskly away, hardly taking notice of the people around them. In buses, trains, streetcars and other public places, most people mind their own business, hardly taking notice of what is happening around them. Those who talk, laugh, shout loudly or do anything to break the prevailing peace appear odd to the serious-looking, concentrated and disciplined onlookers around them. German-Buroni would, with all certainty, have loved it here.

9

My first experience of life in a deep freezer

&

I will now turn my attention to the weather, to describe in the best possible manner the type of weather prevailing in this part of our planet.

It may well be an understatement to say that the sun is a scarce commodity in this part of the world. In Germany, in any given year, one rarely experiences up to three months of real sunshine of the type you and I are familiar with. On the contrary, for most part of the year, the weather might be described as anything but fine. A stormy and wet day may precede days of fog which in turn could herald the coming of snow. And the sun? One can wait months on end in vain for it to bid residents the first hello of the year.

If it had been possible for you to visit here, I would have arranged for your visit to take place during summer. It is only during that time of the year that one can hope for regular sunshine. Even then there is no guarantee of that happening. Indeed, there have been years during which the sun has disappointed its fans and admirers, when it barely lets its presence be felt in the season it would normally be expected to shine.

The summer season ends in mid-September, to be followed by autumn. In autumn the relatively high summer temperatures begin to fall steadily. The sun, when it does appear, persists for only a short time.

At about five in the evening it gradually turns dark—and the darkness persists till about eight the next morning! The leaves of most plants turn yellow and fall at this time of year.

By the onset of winter in late December, most trees have completely shed their leaves. For individuals like you and me who grew up in a hot climate, the winter season could be an unpleasant time were we to live here. It is a time of terrible cold, a season in which the whole visible world seems to exist under the conditions prevailing in a deep freezer.

At this stage I shall turn your attention back to a period about twenty years ago. At that time certain traders from the district capital used to visit our village with vans that one might describe as "cold houses". Such delivery vans were filled with frozen fish that their owners sold to the residents of the settlements they visited. We termed the frozen fish "iced-fish".

You always had difficulty pronouncing English words that had been absorbed into our local language. As in this case, too, calling the fish "iced-fish" was a challenge for you. After much effort on the part of the several "junior academics" you knew, who saw it as a duty to help you pronounce "iced-fish", you finally settled on something that sounded like "ayerese"! You may recall how cold the "ayerese" we bought from the mobile cold-storage units really was! If so, you are not far from getting an idea of how cold the winters here actually are!

Those born into these severe weather conditions seem to have grown used to it. Naturally, there is still the need for them to put on suitable clothing to cope with the low temperatures.

Someone like me who has come to regard the sun as a daily companion had a tough time adjusting to the new conditions. During my first winter experience I had no choice but to wrap my body in as much clothing as I could lay my hands on. The clothes I ended up wearing before I dared venture into the freezing world outside may well amount to about three times what the average citizen here needed! On extraordinarily cold days, I used to put on so much clothing that I could have been likened to an astronaut on a mission in outer space!

In time my body managed somehow to adapt to the changed environmental situation. At present I can manage with fewer clothes than I used to put on in the initial stages. I have the feeling, though, that I will never altogether adjust to the winters here—not in the way a person born here probably can.

In your case I have strong doubts that you would ever survive a winter here! What else should I expect of a person who even seemed to freeze during our local harmattan season—the period around Christmas and early January when cold dry winds from the Sahara Desert blow over most of Ghana, causing the night and early morning temperatures to fall as low as around 20 degrees Celsius (plus)!

It is superfluous to draw your attention to the fact that it is not only the world outside that gets cold during the winter season but also the homes as well.

Long ago residents here made use of simple methods like setting ablaze firewood to keep themselves warm over the winter season. At present more modern heating systems, which help to maintain suitable room temperatures during winter, are widespread here. Another good example of a world of contradictions! While a place like Mpintimpi can become so hot that residents feel they are suffocating under the effect of the terrible heat to the extent of deserting their rooms in the night to sleep under the open skies, in this part of the world one has to spend money to get one's home heated at certain times of the year to avoid being frozen!

During the winter season it is not only cold; for the most part it is also dark. One barely notices traces of the sun in the skies during the day. The day is short, the night is long; nature appears to be undergoing a long period of rest.

One aspect of winter that fascinates me still is the snow that usually pours down from heaven at this time of year. How do I paint a picture of it to your imagination? You may think of a pure white wet substance made up of flakes, almost like feathers raining down from the skies. After a heavy downpour of snow, or snowfall, the whole world is covered by a thick carpet of the white substance.

The world around is then very beautiful to behold. From the rooftops of buildings, from the leaves and branches of trees on the fields right up to the mountains and down to the valleys, the whole world around seems everywhere to be covered with the crystal white substance.

The worst of the winter lasts from late December to the last weeks of March. Towards the end of March, the sun that seemed to have deserted the inhabitants here, begins gradually to make its influence felt.

Spring, considered by many to be the most beautiful season of the year, arrives at last! The plants that went through most of autumn and the whole of winter devoid of their leaves begin to blossom. In due time their flowers begin to smile to refresh the hearts and minds of the human inhabitants. Although spring generally is not as warm as summer, the later part of it can turn hot.

Summer, the season usually associated with bright sunny days, finally sets in towards the end of June.

From all that you have heard in regard to the weather prevailing here, you may now begin to understand why many a resident here seems to want to worship the sun when it shines. It was only after I had lived here for a while that I began to comprehend the wisdom in the English saying we were taught at school—make hay while the sun shines!

How often did we complain at home about the ever-present heat! Often in the midst of the cold winter here, I wished I could be back at home enjoying the beautiful African sun. At such moments the wisdom behind the Twi saying—many a husband fails to realise how valuable his wife is until he loses her—came home forcefully to me.

10

Family narrowly defined

❧

Having touched on the weather, I will now turn my attention to the family set-up of the population here. In modern western society the concept of family contrasts greatly with what you are used to at home. It can be described as "nuclear," involving a married couple and their child or children. Members of the nuclear family unit may maintain contacts with their other close relatives—parents, brothers, sisters, cousins, etc. Such contacts tend to be sparse and restricted to important occasions, such as birthdays, Christmas and New Year's Day, or in the event of the death of a member.

Children usually stay at home with their parents until they turn 18 years. Beyond that age many leave home to fend for themselves. Others stay on until they learn a trade or complete their university education.

It is true that at our end many a child may not be in a hurry to seek an independent life away from the controlling eyes of parents—partly as a result of strong family ties, partly as a result of the fact that such young adults may find it financially difficult living on their own away from home. Many such young persons consequently may not be in a hurry to leave home to settle on their own.

The young adults here do not generally experience such financial constraints. Even should that be the case, my observation is that those concerned generally tend to have a stronger desire to leave home, nevertheless, to fend for themselves as compared to their peers at home. Sometime I can only shake my head when I observe the craving of many a young adult here to leave the parental home, some of those homes mansions that could still offer them abundant space, to seek their own accommodation. Apparently the only thing that matters to such individuals is the feeling of independence and therefore an escape from direct parental influence.

11

A strange recipe for overcoming boredom

R esidents here generally live an isolated life, in contrast to what you are used to at home. Several factors account for this development. Among them are the following:

In the Aburokyire setting, a typical flat has a kitchen, a bath or shower and toilet facilities. This helps make the inhabitant of such apartments independent of one another.

Added to this is the fact that people here have storage facilities such as refrigerators and deep freezers in their apartments or homes that enable them to store enough foodstuffs at home to last for some time. This means that people who are retired from work, unemployed, or who are on holiday or in a situation which does not require him or her to leave home every day, have the benefit of being able to remain indoors throughout a particular day or even over a couple of days, should they choose to do so.

In Germany, in order possibly to keep intruders and thieves away and also to prevent the cold from entering homes in winter, the main gates leading to almost every building are kept shut most of the time. Usually, an electronic-locking system is installed at the entrances to almost every building. Apart from the main gate, the doors to each flat in an apartment block are also fitted with electric opening and locking systems.

Assuming you visited me and we decided to call on a friend of mine living in a building on the other side of my street, with all certainty, the main gate to the building would be locked when we arrived there.

"How do we get in?" you would wonder.

"Wait and see," I would reply.

Just beside the door our eyes would be drawn to a board on which the names of all the inhabitants in the eight-storey building are engraved. Patiently I would go through the list to look for the name of my friend. After I had figured it out, I would press a knob beside the name.

"What are you up to?" you would inquire.

"I'm ringing the bell in his room."

"Really?" Your eyes would be filled with amazement.

A few seconds later a voice would sound through the microphone at the gate:

"*Who is there, please?*"

"It's me—Robert!"

Moments later a shrill noise would be heard at the gate. Hearing this, I would push on the gate. Lo and behold, it would have opened before your eyes!

"My goodness, I'm seeing and experiencing strange things today!" might well be your reaction.

On entering the building, you would probably expect to walk straight into the room of my friend. No, that would not be the case. Although we were indeed in the apartment block, we would still have to go through a process similar to what we went through at the main gate.

I have just taken you through the basic opening and locking systems found in almost every home here. Some house-owners, especially the wealthy ones, may go further, to the extent of installing sophisticated security systems to keep intruders away from their homes.

As a result of what I have just described to you, it would be inadvisable for one to attempt to undertake an unannounced visit to a neighbour. Someone like yourself who is inclined to visit her immediate neighbours regularly, could not, under the conditions prevailing here, just get up and walk to the door of a neighbour with the intention of just saying "hello." No you would need to call the individual first to give him or her a foreknowledge of your intention to visit.

It is largely true that here there is barely any contact between neighbours—yes, even between those who share the same floor of an apartment block! The little exchanges that may occur—if at all—hardly go beyond casual greetings like "hello!" and "how are you?" Such sporadic exchanges usually occur when, once in a blue moon, chance permits the ways of those involved to cross at the staircase, outside or inside the lift, at the main gate to the house, and so forth.

Can you imagine a situation at home where death in an apartment block with several tenants can go undetected for days, weeks, even months? Even in a city like Accra, where one could talk of a degree of anonymity between neighbours, such a situation could hardly arise. Even in the very rare instances where a person in Ghana lives alone, the absence of that person over a period of a few days would strike the attention of others in no time and lead them to inquire after the individual involved.

The media here recently carried a report of someone whose death went undetected for almost a year. It was not a case involving someone living alone in an isolated building. No—according to the report, the person involved lived in a large apartment building housing several others. Questioned on the matter, the answers of the immediate neighbours of the deceased ranged from "we assumed he had gone on holiday," "we thought he had gone to visit a cousin living several kilometres away," to "we thought he had been admitted to hospital."

"How did they come to estimate the approximate time of death?" you might ask. The investigating officers based it on two factors. They took into account the date the last TV programme guide they saw in the living room was issued and also the dates stamped on the letters that had piled up in his letterbox to determine when the earliest among them might have been delivered.

If I had not been to Aburokyire I would never have known how it feels for one to spend several days in one's own room without anyone to talk to. That is not to say that there were no immediate neighbours in the apartment block where I lived. Yes, indeed, there were several other tenants—directly on my floor as well as in the building as a whole. How could one get access to anyone there when everyone, including myself, was locked up in his or her various rooms?

To release some of the tension that used to build up in me as I spent my time alone in my "cage," I would from time to time stand before a mirror built to the one of the doors to my wardrobe, look at my reflection in it and begin to crack jokes with myself! Loneliness and boredom, mother, threatened, seriously to drive your son crazy.

12

An ex-husband threatened with bankruptcy

&

All marriages here in Germany are registered in court. The traditional system of marriage as practised at home is not found here.

In the same way that all marriages here are sealed under the long arm of the law, divorces are executed also under its realms. The rate of divorce in western society is quite high.

As you are aware, in our society most wives depend on their husbands for financial existence. Love for a man does not in many cases play the primary role in a woman's decision to marry a man. Rather, it is the ability of the future husband to provide for her financially that counts. In this regard many a woman may close her eyes to the fact that the would-be husband happens to be a person who already has a wife or who may even have several wives. It is on the basis of the above that one can understand the reluctance of many women at home to opt for divorce.

On the contrary, many a western woman is financially self-sufficient. In such a situation personal affection for the individual can be the deciding factor for a woman to marry him. In the same vein financial independence might lead a woman to leave a marriage without being overly concerned about subsequent financial repercussions. One might even dare assert that divorce, while not ruining her financially, might even bring her financial gain in the light of what I will tell you in due course regarding the payment of alimony.

The first step a person seeking divorce in this society takes is to contact a solicitor; the legal expert in turn forwards an application to the appropriate court. In Germany the law basically requires the couple to be separated for a minimum of a year before divorce can be executed. The period of separation might be extended an additional two years should one of the parties involved refuse to approve of the dissolution of the matrimonial bond. After a maximum of three years separation, however, divorce is normally carried out even if one party disapproves of it.

Divorce can be quite an expensive matter here. This is particularly the case when the couple involved is wealthy and substantial property needs to be shared between the two. According to my information, the fee demanded by a lawyer is usually directly proportionate to the value of property involved. The divorce hearings take place in special courts. In addition to meeting the bills of their lawyers, the couple concerned are also usually required to bear the cost of the court sitting, or sittings, as the case may be.

In this society, divorce does not usually end the responsibility of marriage couples to one another. Depending on the income levels of the two individuals involved, the court could ask one party to pay alimony to the other. Such regular monetary remunerations, usually on a monthly basis, can go on indefinitely.

They can be reviewed should the recipient re-marry, or take up a job which brings him or her substantial income, or if the party making the regular payments finds himself or herself in a situation where he or she may no longer be earning enough to cater for himself or herself.

By virtue of their biological endowment, women have to bear the larger responsibility of caring for a child. The birth of a child can lead some to give up their jobs. Some may return after a while to re-occupy their positions; others never return. In a divorce sitting the courts take all these factors into account. Partly as a result of all this, it usually happens that ex-husbands are called upon to pay alimony to their former wives and not the other way round.

"An ex-husband paying for the upkeep of a former wife!" I hear you exclaim. "Is that fiction or reality?" you ask. That, mother, is reality! Unlike the situation at home, particularly in the rural areas where a husband can choose to send his wife away without caring in the least about the financial repercussions his decision might have on the woman concerned, over here the law has the power to intervene, to cause such a person to feel the financial pinch of his decision.

Matters in regard to alimony are considered independently of the arrangement with respect to the upkeep of the child or children involved. So long as the offspring from a marriage have not attained an age where they can fend for themselves, the parents, in most cases, the fathers, have to pay for their upkeep.

At this point I want to narrate the experience of an acquaintance of mine, a citizen of this country, in regard to such matters. His first marriage broke down after a few years. They had two children. The divorce ruling required him not only to pay a specified amount of money every month for the upkeep of his children but in addition to make a specified monthly remission to his former wife by way of alimony. The two children, both of a very tender age, were placed under the custody of their mother. He was permitted access to them only at specified times, and only after prior consultations with his former wife in regard to an appointment.

My acquaintance went on to tell me that as a result of his experience from his first marriage, he resolved never to re-marry. Someone has said that in life one should never say "never"! The wisdom behind that saying would soon come home to him.

After the stormy winds of his first marriage experience had abated and the last drops from the rain that accompanied it had disappeared in fine sand, he gave his heart a second time to an attractive woman that crossed his path. Soon he was married a second time. Not long after the marriage ceremony it was clear that his wife was going to have a baby. In due course he was indeed congratulating himself for having added an additional head to the world population. The joy of his newfound love as well as the joy arising from the new arrival was short-lived, however.

A couple of years after he married the second time he and his second wife found themselves seated before a judge in a divorce hearing! For the second time he was asked to pay alimony for an ex-wife and also transfer money to her every month for the upkeep of their child.

"At the end of the month I am left with barely enough money to live on," the benighted man lamented. "Oh, poor me! Why, oh why me?"— thus he concluded his story in a mood not devoid of a considerable degree of bitterness.

There is little anyone required by law to pay alimony here can do to avoid payment. In the case of a salary or wage earner, the sum involved is usually deducted at source. The self-employed are made to sign an undertaking promising to fulfil their obligations by making the payments required of them at a specified time every month.

Someone has said that human beings are human beings everywhere! Whereas the majority of those called upon to make such payments fulfil their obligations, others, for reasons that may well not border on affordability, choose to go to any ends to avoid meeting their obligations.

At this point I shall cite a case that appeared in the newspapers in Hanover to illustrate my point. The case involved an engineer who, from all accounts, could not be counted with the poor and needy. Called upon to pay for the upkeep of his former wife and their child in her custody, he decided to give up his business and register as a university student. From thenceforth he refused to make the payments required of him. When the former wife demanded the money due, he countered by pointing out that, being but a poor student, he was himself having difficulties making ends meet. This being the case, how did she expect him to have anything left for others? As might be expected, his ex-wife was not prepared to swallow that argument and initiated steps to fight for her rights! Soon the two former sweethearts were battling each other in court.

It is not only matters such as the above that can make enemies of former lovers. As you and I are only too aware, in our traditional society, many a former husband might claim sole ownership of property that might in all probability have come about as a result of the sweat and hard labour of both parties. From what I have already told you in regard to the situation prevailing here, you will already appreciate that a situation of this nature is unlikely to occur.

While not claiming to be an expert on such complicated matters, my information is that during the divorce proceedings the courts here evaluate the worth of property the two parties share in common. Much care is taken not to overlook anything: from very valuable property—homes, factories, pieces of land, large bank accounts, expensive furniture, etc.—right down to property of much lesser value—sets of cutlery, bed-sheets, pillow cases, etc.—every item is meticulously listed.

The pets of the separating couple can also be a point of contention during some divorce hearings. I have indeed read and heard about instances where after all other issues pertaining the divorce have been settled, the issue as to which party gets custody of a family pet has led to disputes, sometimes prolonged ones.

As to be expected, the welfare of the children of a couple seeking divorce receives important priority in the divorce proceedings. This is particularly so when the children involved are young. During the divorce hearing(s) the court rules as to which of the two individuals involved gets custody of the children. In reaching their decisions, the executioners of the legislations of the land take into consideration, among others, the age of the child or children involved, the background of the parents, the family environment, etc.

In line with the Twi proverb "It is the mother hen that knows the best food for her chicks", the courts usually place the child or children under the custody of their mothers.

The individual to whom custody of the children is entrusted is usually also granted the sole right of decision-making on their behalf until they attain the age where they can, by law, assume that responsibility. In certain instances both parents are made to share that right equally.

Matters do not end there; the court also rules on issues such as how often and for how long the child or children may visit the other parent who was denied custody. Extra arrangements are also made in regard to which of the two former lovers gets access to their child or children on special occasions such as Christmas, New Year's Day, Easter, school holidays, etc. For example, the child or children may spend Christmas with one parent and New Year's Day with the other; travel with one parent on the summer holidays of a particular year and with the other on a subsequent year. Both parties make a commitment to abide by the settlement.

The one entrusted with the children must allow the other side to pick them up from time to time in accordance with the ruling and not place undue impediments in the way. The other side of the coin is also true. When the other party picks up the child or children, he or she must make it a point to return them within the stipulated time. Failure to adhere to the spirit of the ruling can lead the other partner to fight for his or her rights in court, a situation that can lead to the imposition of sanctions. There have been instances when the courts have even gone so far as to place a complete ban on contacts between parent and child.

"How can little children become used to the situation you have just described?" you may ask. The impression I have is that many a person here thinks the way you do—namely, that such arrangements could have an adverse effect on the well-being of the child. The decision-makers seem, however, to be at a loss as to how best to get around the problem. They seem to have resigned themselves to the fact that there is nothing else they can do to maintain a certain degree of social peace—perhaps the due price needed to be paid by a highly sophisticated society populated by individuals highly aware of their rights under existing laws.

These arrangements are not devoid of human tragedies, some of which might well be described as catastrophic. The media recently ran a report of an incident that sent the tears streaming from my eyes. The tragic story involved a father of two little children who committed suicide by jumping in front of an approaching train. Before that, he killed his two little children. In line with the divorce arrangement he had picked them up from their mother to interact with them for a while. Apparently he could not come to terms with the divorce and his subsequent separation from the children.

13

Okwonko yearning for the days when men were men

※

Several years ago, a movement that aimed at fighting for equal rights for women in Germany and the West in general got underway. Today many a woman living in western societies feels emancipated. The extent to which a woman in such a society would want the "rules and regulations" guiding the emancipation of the sexes to be implemented in the married setting depends of course on their natural inclination.

Some want to implement the concept of the emancipation of sexes right into the marital home. As far as such women are concerned, every assignment to be performed in the home should be carried out equally between the two parties in the union.

In some homes the role of the sexes, as you know it, is almost reversed. In such instances, from decisions involving how money is spent to that of choosing the colour of furniture fit for the living room, right down to those involving the best way to raise the children, everyone looks up to Eve for the final word. Eve may also leave Adam to perform all the household chores. On the rare occasions when she decides to do the cooking herself, she is sure to insist that whatever additional work is left to be done in the home—washing, cleaning, ironing, putting the children to bed, etc.—should be performed by the other adult in the relationship.

When we were at the second cycle school, one of the books we used for the English Literature class was *Things Fall Apart* by the renowned Nigerian writer Chinua Achebe. The main figure in the book, Okonkwo, was known to rule his home with an iron hand. Should he ever have the opportunity to visit the family setting I have just described, he would with all certainty yearn for the days when, in line with his thinking, "men were men."

One may also come across women, who, while aware of their emancipated status, do not insist on applying the "rules" of emancipation at home. Such women, apparently, seem to be satisfied with the fact that they have their loving husbands around them who, should the need arise, will be prepared to assist them keep the home.

Within the two extremes are found all possible variations—ranging from the strictly democratic home setting where all decisions to be taken have first to be debated upon, sometimes for hours, by both parties involved, right down to the situation where husband and wife, though sharing the same walls of the home, live almost independent lives apart from each other. A stranger to the home might well wonder if the two were indeed husband and wife!

Thus far I have tried to paint a picture of the situation of the western woman in the home setting. What does the situation look like when it comes to the place of work? In theory, based on the provisions of the law, the women in this society are guaranteed equal opportunities vis-à-vis their male counterparts in regard to education, work, as well as voting rights. In practice though, discrepancies to the favour of the male worker still exist in some spheres of life. For example a male worker is likely to earn more than his female counterpart performing the same type of job.

14

Few children here, more children there

Y ou gave birth to eleven children, three of whom passed away at birth or shortly thereafter. Your example is a reflection of the general situation pertaining at home, at least for women of your generation,

The society in the West has developed to the other extreme! Statistics show that on the average, each woman in Germany gives birth to less than two children during her lifetime. That may come as a surprise to someone like you. Indeed, over here you could come across some young people who might tell you with all conviction that they have decided never to give birth to any child at all.

Should you go further to inquire from such individuals the reasons for their decision, you might hear arguments like the following: "I have come to that conclusion because I want to enjoy as much of this life as possible. Should I give birth to children I would be restricted in my movements. No, I do not want any interference in my personal freedom." "Ma'am," another might add, "there are already too many people populating our planet. What is the need for me to add a couple more to the number?" Yet another person might point to the fact that a lot of children in the society leave their parents in their old age alone to fend for themselves. "If that's the fate of those who sacrificed to deliver and raise children, why the need for me to give birth to children who might treat me likewise?"

Of course there are exceptions to every rule. Although they make up a small minority, some couples here also give birth to many children—three, four and more. In some rare cases there have been reports of some giving birth to as many as ten or more children!

Those who dare swim against the tide of society in such a manner must be prepared, at least in Germany, to face the scorn of many. The problem of such large families may begin when they go on a walk on the street, when they board public transport, when they go shopping, or when they visit other public places. On such occasions, many who come across them may look at them with scorn, as if to say to them: "Look how irresponsible you are! Why the need for such a large family?!"

Should such a family decide to look for suitable accommodation, they are likely to experience, once more, the antipathy of their fellow citizens towards such large families. Indeed, many house owners in Germany feel reluctant to rent their flats out to families with three or more children.

This could be the direct result of the house owners' personal aversion towards such families. Such property owners might well be considering their own financial interests, for it is no secret that many a tenant here may not want to be neighbour to a family with many children. The argument such persons present is that such children tend to be noisy, a fact that could deprive them of the necessary peace and quiet they need to make them feel comfortable in their home.

Those who allow such families to move into their homes thus risk driving away tenants already living there as well as potential ones wishing to move in.

There have been instances where tenants have taken their landlords to court to ask the courts to effect a reduction in their rents because a family with a large number of children had moved into the building. The presence of such children in their vicinity—children who in reality may not be noisy—could be regarded by the complainant as tantamount to a reduction in the value of their apartment.

In the compounds surrounding many homes in Germany, for example, there are often plates and boards bearing the following inscription:

"Children are prohibited from playing here!"

Parents are advised to take such warnings seriously, for they risk being prosecuted should their children break such regulations.

I once read a newspaper report of a dispute of that nature. Surrounding a big apartment block was a field that had formerly served as a playground for the children living there. Apparently as a result of pressure from tenants who felt disturbed by children playing there, the owner of the house decided overnight to turn the playground to a "non-playground." Accordingly a signpost drawing the attention of the public to the change was put in place.

The three sons of a couple living there, apparently not bothered by the altered situation, continued to play their favourite game of football on the field, just like they'd been doing previously. They probably underestimated the determination of the property owner to enforce the regulations governing his premises. They were soon to find out otherwise, for the owner reacted promptly by taking their parents to court.

The presiding judge, on his part, at least on the basis of the judgement passed, might well be described as someone who seemed unfriendly towards children. Indeed, he threatened to fine the parents around half a million German marks should they fail to make their children comply with the rules and regulations governing the home! To give you an idea of the scale of the amount of money involved—half a million German marks is money that would be able not only to take care of the whole population of Mpintimpi for a whole lifetime, but also that of their children's children!

Another factor that restricts the free movement of children here is the ever-present busy traffic. Owing to the large volume of traffic found here, there is an increased danger of children being knocked down by vehicles. Partly as a result of this, children living in this part of the world usually can play only in playgrounds specially built for that purpose.

At this stage, while I'm dealing with the issue of children and the attitude of society towards them, I also want to consider some social factors prevailing here that also account for the reluctance of some individuals to give birth to children.

Our family ties are such that when a woman brings forth a child, at least one female relative from her own family or her partner's readily offers to come and stay with them for a while in order to help them cope with the extra burden. This is generally true even for the urban setting.

In the village setting, new mothers are treated like princesses. Almost every member of the extended families of the new parents as well as other members of the community in general do their best to assist them. All that the new mother needs do in the initial stages is breastfeed her child. All the other chores of the home—washing the baby, washing the clothes of mother and child, fetching water from the well or the stream, cooking, etc.—are performed by willing helpers.

Indeed, a new mother in the village, particularly if it happens to be her first birth, does practically nothing during the first several weeks after delivery.

In the Aburokyire society, few new mothers have that luxury. On the whole, such mothers are left alone with their husbands, if they have any, to care for their babies. The new father, should he be working, might usually expect his employer to allow him only a few days off. Thereafter he has to return to work or risk losing his job.

"Why don't some of their relatives come round to assist them?" you might ask. Some indeed do. These are exceptional cases, however. In Aburokyire society many relatives may be busy working or seeking work. As a result they may not have any time available to assist such a relative.

The need to work and the resulting lack of time are not the only limiting factors that prevent relatives to come to the aid of such mothers, however. This is a sophisticated society. The advancement of society, in turn, has had its repercussions on the thinking and deeds of the individuals living in it. Certain factors that individuals living at Mpintimpi, for example, take for granted are viewed differently here.

Let us assume, for example, that the grandmother of the young mother here volunteers to visit her granddaughter who has just given birth to a child with the aim of helping her cope with the stress of the first few weeks. Issues that in our traditional context would not pose any hindrances, could, in this society, be allowed to block the good-intentions of the elderly lady. For example, the granddaughter and her husband might raise the question of accommodation.

"Where will Grandma sleep on her arrival?" the two young parents might ask.

"Our bed-sit flat consists of a small living room and just one bedroom that serves our needs as well as that of the child. If only we had an additional room to accommodate her!"

Who would possibly want to raise such an issue at our end? Even a flat made up only of a living and a bedroom would in all probability be considered adequate. The visitor might well be satisfied with a blanket spread on the floor of the sitting room for her to sleep on! The thought of being able to help her grand daughter in her moment of need would be enough to dissipate all feelings of inconvenience.

In Germany and in many other countries in Aburokyire relatives rarely settle on such a simple solution. While many a relative wanting to go to the aid of the young mother might in fact be prepared to sleep on the floor, the beneficiaries of the goodwill of their relative might actually object to the arrangement on the grounds that the expensive carpet in the living room might be damaged in the process!

But let us assume that the sleeping arrangements were not a hindrance and that the mother or grandmother of the young mother came to help. At home your children gave you a free hand to handle your grandchildren the way you thought best. It never occurred to any of them that someone like you, a veteran in the affairs of child delivery and care, could be wrong in your methods regarding things like the proper way to hold the baby whilst washing it, the proper way to apply cream or lotion to the body of the baby, or the proper way to feed it.

The situation is not that straightforward here. Over here arguments may well arise between you and your daughter (or daughter-in-law) in regard to the best way to treat *her* child. She could tell you that she had also informed herself in detail (in a book, probably) as to the best way to nurse a baby, and she would want to do things "by the book." She may insist you do things the way she tells you. After all, you have come to help her with *her* baby.

In the course of your stay, so many arguments on how best to handle the little baby might creep in, to the extent that you would sooner rather than later decide the best way out was for you to leave your daughter's residence well ahead of schedule!

As the above example illustrates, our idea that a child is born into a family, not born, as it were, only to her parents but rather to the whole extended family, a view that allows all members of the family to have free access to the child, would sound very strange to many people here. Some parents here even go to the extent of refusing to entrust their little ones to any third person, even a close relative or close friend.

15

Happy birthday to you!

❧

Y ou do not stand alone in regard to ignorance in the matter of your exact date of birth. Indeed, millions of residents at home and elsewhere in the developing countries of the world share your fate as well. Even to this day, a considerable number of births occurring in many parts of the world are not recorded. From time immemorial residents in this part of the world have kept records of important events, including those involving the dates on which their children were born.

Currently almost every birth that occurs here takes place either in a hospital or in a maternity home. The few births that occur at home or elsewhere, apart from the above-named places, are reported to the responsible authorities soon after birth. Records on births are kept right down to the very minute the newborn arrives in the world. A corresponding certificate indicating the date and place of birth as well as the names of the parents involved is issued not long after the birth of an individual.

In this society one's date of birth accompanies one throughout life. Whatever documents the person fills, whatever admissions the individual seeks, whatever position the person applies for, the person involved is required to give the date of birth. The world here may well cease to function entirely, or at least not properly, should an end be made to the constant reference to the dates of births of its residents.

One would naturally not expect people who have no records of their dates of births to mark the annual return or anniversary of such events.

That is exactly the case. When was the last time we heard or saw an individual at Mpintimpi throw a party to mark his or her birthday? In just the same way we never came across any parent there who organised a party to mark the birthday of a child.

The situation in the towns and cities, in particular among the rich and educated, could be different from that prevailing in the rural areas. Indeed, many such persons may celebrate their birthdays and those of their children. Still, one can safely say that celebrating birthdays is not a universal aspect of our culture.

The situation is different here. From the cradle right to the grave, the great majority of residents here, or their parents, tend to celebrate their birthdays. Almost every parent here organises a birthday party for their little one.

The first birthday of a child is usually accorded special significance. Later, when children attend day-care or kindergarten or begin their schooling, the custom is for them to invite their peers to join them in the celebration.

Many an individual here attaches special importance to the 18th birthday. As I mentioned earlier, it is at that age that the individual officially becomes an adult. From then on the person can, within the realms of the law, make decisions without the need to consult anyone else—not even his or her parents. Consequently many an individual wants to mark the occasion in a special manner.

Elsewhere, I did talk about the fact that many elderly citizens here live on their own. Come their birthdays, however, especially when it involves so-called round figures—50, 60, 70, 80, 90 or even 100—relatives, some of whom they have not seen for months, pour into their homes to congratulate them. The guests usually do not arrive empty-handed but rather bring with them birthday cards, bouquets of flowers as well as various kinds of presents.

For a while the world of family members, who under normal circumstances may have little or no contact with each other, is all harmony. The visitors gather around Grandma or Grandpa's dining table to eat delicious meals, enjoy wonderful cakes, drink coffee or/and tea and in some cases champagne, whisky, etc. The rare get-together of family members offers them a wonderful opportunity for lively conversations, discussions, joke cracking, etc. Some re-tell important and sometimes dramatic moments from the family's past. The get-together lasts for a while.

Soon, however, one guest after another begins to take a glance at his or her watch.

"Grandma," one of them might begin, "unfortunately I have to leave now. You are aware that tomorrow is another working day. I have to rise early, at the latest at five, to get ready for work. All the best, Grandma, till next time!"

Moments after the sound of the departing guest is no longer heard on the staircase, a second person might be heard:

"Mutti, I beg to leave as well. I am expecting an important call in about an hour's time. I need to be at home by then."

And so one after the other the guests leave for their homes. Very soon Grandma or Grandpa's wonderful day will be nearing its end. In due course Grandma or Grandpa will be left alone at home to face the hard realities of life and probably to reflect on the factors that led to a situation where many residents here, willingly or unwillingly, leave their elderly relatives on their own.

If you happened to visit here during your lifetime, one of the questions you would have been asked on a regular basis would have been: "How old are you, please?" That would especially be the case should you begin to develop a close relationship with someone here. The next question would likely be: "When is your next birthday?"

Initially I was irritated by such questions. I wondered why, for heaven's sake, my acquaintance was being so inquisitive. After I had replied to the question, I expected the person to switch to other matters. As it turned out, I was at that time not conversant with the thinking of the society here.

When the question resurfaced at a time when my birthday happened to be around the corner, the questioner was likely to go further and inquire whether I intended to throw a party to celebrate the occasion, and if that were the case, whether I had any special wishes that I would want to be fulfilled on that day.

The new arrival from Africa was surprised that the newfound friend seemed to be so inquisitive. Now that he has lived here long enough to realise the extent to which friends and other acquaintances may wish to go to look for a suitable gift to gladden the hearts of individuals on the occasion of their birthdays, he now, in retrospect, understands the attitude of some of his early friends.

Even if, for one reason or the other, one fails to invite a friend or acquaintance on the occasion of one's birthday, many of them would still want to send a card or make a telephone call to congratulate the person.

Being constantly reminded of how old one is can sometimes bring with it psychological problems, however. This is particularly so in the society prevailing here, in which one generally tends to worship the young and attractive, the strong and athletic, the dynamic and energetic, and whatever else one would choose to describe those enjoying the prime of their lives.

The moment a former young and attractive model, for example, becomes middle-aged and grey hair begins to replace the once attractive blonde hair, and the once youthful skin begins to wrinkle, few, if any, of her former admirers, take any more notice of her. Why should they, when in the meantime society might have long discovered a new idol whose turn has come to be adored and worshipped?! Some of such former heroes of society, former famous stars of the world both near and far, never manage to come to terms with reality.

16

When the grey hairs begin to appear

A Twi proverb has it that the person who nursed an individual to enable that person to develop teeth deserves to be reciprocated by the beneficiary of his or her care when the time comes for him or her to lose teeth. In keeping with that saying, sons and daughters in our society generally see it as their responsibility to care for their aging parents.

Care for the elderly is not restricted to one's parents only; elderly members of the extended family who do not have their own children or whose children for one reason or another are not in a position to do so, are generally catered for by other members of the extended family. In short: our society generally goes to great lengths to assimilate its aging members into its fold.

In the past, the family structure in this society was similar to what you are familiar with—a large family in which more than one generation lived in the same family compound. With the onset of industrialisation, sons and daughters, after they had attained a certain age, left their parents in search of work in the large towns and cities that had begun to spring up.

To meet the demand for homes for the new arrivals, several apartment blocks were erected. In the past the flats in such buildings had several rooms capable of housing a large family. In time, probably in response to the trend of society to give birth to fewer children, the sizes of such flats were reduced. As time progressed, contacts between the sons and daughters who had left the countryside to work in the urban areas and their relations remaining became scanty. With this came the gradual erosion of the close ties between family members in this part of the world.

At the moment the Aburokyire society, Germany being a good example, has developed into a dynamic, achievement-centred, results-orientated one—a fast moving society where only the strong, the active, the good looking, the successful tend to count. On the other hand, the old, the sick, the weak, the handicapped, and all who are incapable of maintaining their balance in this fast moving express train of western life have either to make way for the fittest and strongest or be crushed under the wheels of the gigantic steel colossus of the modern world.

The young and healthy who, on their part, have to struggle hard to find their feet in this very competitive society, find little or no time to care for their aging mothers and fathers. The result is that for the most part the old are left alone to fend for themselves.

Can you imagine a person past the age of eighty years having to live alone, having to perform all household chores—cleaning the home, going shopping, cooking, washing dishes, alone?

Should one have the opportunity to talk to such a person, one might discover that the senior citizen concerned could indeed have several close relatives—children, grand- and even great-grandchildren, some of whom even may happen to live not very far away. The elderly person could develop the conversation further and recall the good old days when he or she was growing up as a child.

"At that time our family ties were strong. The parents of my mother as well as the mother of my father lived with us. My other grandfather was already dead. I was the youngest member of the family. I had six older siblings. It was a wonderful experience growing up in a large family. Things have changed completely, however. Our children these days have become egoistic, to put it mildly. They think only about working to earn money for themselves. They do not want to be burdened by the issues concerning the old. My grandchildren have made it a habit to call on me only when they need something from me! I wish I could spend the rest of my days on earth living within the familiar walls of my home.

I hate the idea of having to move into a home for the elderly. Dear Lord, please spare me that fate!"

The elderly person does not stand alone in her attitude towards the prospect of living in such homes; many a senior would rather die than end up there. Many I have had the opportunity to talk to consider such homes as places where one more or less goes to live out the remainder of one's life, waiting for the inevitable—where the only escape is via the cemetery. The impression I got from such conversations is that many who raised their own children, some of whom might well be in the position to house them, tend to be disappointed, if not embittered, at the prospect of having to go to live in such homes.

What I have described reflects the general situation. As the saying goes, every rule has its exception. Indeed, there are relatives over here who go to great lengths to cater for their elderly parents and other elderly relations, sometimes at the expense even of their own health.

The homes for the elderly, to give them their due, go to considerable lengths to cater for their residents and make them feel as comfortable as possible. My own experience tells me, however, that the staff there are often overburdened by the tedious tasks of nursing the residents, many of whom may be bedridden. This often leaves them with little time to provide the warmth and affection a close relative or friend could offer.

Poor and deprived as you may be back home, your children and other relatives have not deserted you in your old age. At this critical stage of your life you can be sure of the constant company of relatives as well as friends and acquaintances to offer you solidarity in your battle with death. Many people of your age living at this end of our planet, some of whom may have access to considerable wealth can only dream of such a privilege.

Seniors who opt to live alone at home instead of moving to live in such special homes usually have to cope with a host of difficulties in their day-to-day lives. One can see some of them in the supermarkets as they wearily go about their shopping; at the next moment one might find them on the streets as they struggle to transport their shopping bags home.

As if that were not enough! Some unscrupulous individuals take advantage of their precarious situation for their own selfish ends. From time to time the media carry reports of elderly citizens falling victim to such ruthless individuals. Cruel and pitiless thugs who seem to have no sympathy for their helpless victims may rob the senior citizen on the streets of their belongings.

The burglar may take advantage of the failing memories of such seniors to pose as a close or distant relative, a friend or even a social worker who has come to help them. The moment the unsuspecting elderly open their homes to them, they ransack their flats for money and other valuables. Some of the robbers are so unscrupulous they do not refrain from the application of brutal force to achieve their goal. Some seniors have suffered serious injuries or have even died as a result of such attacks.

Old people living on their own usually not only have to cook their own food; many also have to perform other household chores on their own as well. Those who have their spouses alive and healthy try to supplement each other's efforts in line with the saying, "two heads are better than one".

The plight of other elderly citizens battling things on their own is even less enviable. I have witnessed several instances where one of the duo happens to be bedridden. In some instances, the burden of nursing and caring for the bedridden partner is shouldered in the main by the already frail partner!

To be fair to the society, it must be mentioned that the state as well as the several charitable organisations here have developed means to get round some of the above problems. Some seniors, for example, may be reluctant to move to the homes for the elderly, not because they shun them, but rather on financial grounds. For one reason or the other such individuals may not be in a position to pay the monthly fee demanded by the proprietors (it can be quite substantial). In such situations, the state may step in to offer financial assistance.

Special companies and organisations have sprung up to provide services ranging from home-nursing, home meal-delivery, shopping, right down to tidying the homes of the affected for a fee. (Here, too, the fee demanded can add up to substantial amounts.) Those seniors who are not in a position to bear the costs on their own can apply to the state for financial assistance.

What are the resources at the disposal of old people living on their own in times of emergency? As I pointed out earlier, almost everyone in this society possesses a telephone. In case of an emergency they can dial a special number. There are some old people living in their own homes who, because of disease or age, are incapable of performing such a simple action on their own. Never mind—this is a highly developed technological society, as I pointed out earlier. Technology has developed a solution to the problem by putting in place a system that makes it possible for the elderly persons to draw attention to their plight without the need even to dial a number!

This is how the system works: A special device is installed in the room of the bedridden person. The device is connected to the home telephone. A small gadget that serves as a remote control capable of activating the device is hung around the neck of the person involved or fixed in a position that permits the affected person free access at any time. In an emergency all that the individual need do is to press a button on the remote control. This sets a chain reaction in motion. First, the home telephone is activated to automatically dial the number of the care company responsible for the individual. Such centres have surveillance staff on duty around the clock. The attendant on duty will then communicate with the affected individual. The bedridden person needs only to speak in the air; the device then carries the message over.

Even if the caller is no longer capable of speaking, once he or she activates the device, the staff automatically know from whom the ringing originates and quickly despatch personnel to the person's home. To avoid a situation in which the death of their client might go undetected for days, the bedridden person is requested to routinely press a knob first thing on waking up every morning.

Not every elderly citizen living alone has access—or wishes to have access—to such facilities, however. Apart from not having the substantial fees often required for such facilities, many a senior citizen, in particular those who are not bedridden and are capable, if only with difficulty, of living a certain degree of independent life, may not see the need for them.

The unpredictable nature of medical emergencies may sometimes catch such individuals on the wrong footing, leaving them with insufficient time to reach for their telephones. Should such medical emergencies result in the death of the affected person, it could take days if not weeks, in some cases even months, for the passing away to be detected.

I shall close this chapter by telling you some of the experiences I had as a junior doctor on the surgical ward at the district hospital at Helmstedt, a large town about one hundred kilometres to the east of Hanover.

On a regular basis we admitted elderly patients, the majority of them aged 80 years and above who had sustained fractures to their hips, mostly from falling. After successfully undergoing treatment, the time finally came for them to be discharged. The issue of where to send them could engage the staff on the ward for several hours. In several instances we got to know that the affected patients, prior to their admission, had been living on their own at home. Until then only with considerable difficulty had they managed to brave the storms of life. As a result of the trauma, the surgery and the subsequent hospitalisation, this would no longer be possible. The responsibility for the staff on the ward, therefore, was to ensure the individual was discharged to an environment where he or she would be catered for.

How did we go about finding a solution to the problem? First, we tried to establish contacts with the close relatives of the patient to find out whether any of them would be prepared to receive the affected person at home. Some of the responses we got were as follows:

"I surely would like to help. Unfortunately I leave home very early in the morning to work all day; how can I care for anyone under such circumstances?"

"I am already overburdened caring for my little children; how can I place an additional burden on my shoulders?"

"We do not have enough space at home to accommodate an additional head."

Even some relatives who lived with the affected persons before their injuries refused to accept them back on grounds that they would not be able to cope with the additional workload.

Often, after spending several minutes making several calls to relatives, we were left with no alternative but to make arrangements for the affected person to be admitted to a home.

One elderly female patient was so disappointed at the refusal of her son to admit her back home that she fell into a deep depression from which she never recovered and died a few days after the news reached her. Before her death she confided to some staff members the reason for her disappointment. Several years earlier, her son had promised her to allow her to live in the family home till her death. On the basis of that promise she had prematurely transferred ownership of the property from herself to him.

17

"Lead us not into temptation"

❧

Food not only abounds in the society where I live at present, they are sold at prices that is generally affordable to the average resident.

Indeed one can without exaggeration state that the abundance and affordability of food in this society makes the risk of residents overfeeding themselves very real indeed. The world, mother, seems only capable of existing within extreme parameters for whereas residents in some parts of the world barely obtain enough food to feed themselves, a fact that leads some even to die of starvation as well as other diseases associated with malnutrition, elsewhere on the same planet, residents have so much to eat that some die of diseases related directly or indirectly to overeating!

Contrary to the situation prevailing in Ghana whereby basic foodstuff—plantain, maize, cassava, yams, etc.—are distributed mainly by "market mammies," over here that function is assumed by special supermarkets. These shops, dear mother, do indeed deserve the accolade: "super"! You should see some of them for yourself!

The moment someone like you, deprived for the most of your life of an adequate food supply, stepped into a typical supermarket here, the cells in your mouth responsible for the production of saliva would immediately spring into action to pour large quantities of the fluid into your mouth. Indeed, the sight of the abundant and appealing food items crammed onto the shelves would leave those dutiful cells no other option other than to initiate the appropriate steps in anticipation of the privilege, at long last, of assisting in the digestion and absorption into the body system of those wonderful foodstuffs your eyes beheld!

You might want to know whether some of the foodstuffs we are used to—yams, plantains, bananas, oranges, pineapples, etc.—are also available here. These types of crops that require a certain amount of sunshine to grow cannot survive through the cold winters here. They are however imported from elsewhere to satisfy the demand for them, especially from those from Ghana, Africa and other countries in the tropics where such crops are grown.

The indigenous population usually prefer locally-grown foodstuffs—potatoes, cereals, cabbage, spinach, apples, pears, etc.—which are produced in large quantities by local farmers.

At home chicken is generally considered a delicacy because most people cannot afford to serve it at their tables regularly. Consequently chicken is usually reserved for special occasions such as Christmas and Easter. Following on that thinking, one might as well regard every day of the year as Christmas here!

Indeed, chicken abounds and is sold at a price that, theoretically, could enable the average citizen here to consume a whole chicken each day of the year! Many of our nationals, when they first arrive here, take advantage of the situation and consume as much chicken as possible in the initial stages. Soon, however, many come to realise there is no way they can keep pace with the supply from the farmers who produce large quantities of the birds daily! Chicken is not the only bird on sale in large quantities in the supermarkets; turkey and geese also abound and are offered at prices the average citizen can afford.

When one becomes fed up with eating birds, one can turn to other types of meat products like pork, beef, and lamb. These are also in plentiful supply and generally affordable to the average citizen.

The wishes of the consumer more inclined towards fish are also met. Among the large variety of fish on sale in the supermarkets are: herrings, tuna, salmon and mackerel; these are sold fresh, roasted or toasted.

Also on sale are large quantities of canned food products of all types and kinds: beans, tomatoes, sardines, mackerel, beef, pork, etc.

Other food items abound: dairy products, eggs, cheese, butter, as well as baked products, bread of all types and makes, and cakes of all types and varieties.

I nearly forgot to mention chocolate! Chocolate is a favourite food item for many a resident here. Do you know the main raw material used in the production of chocolate? Cocoa beans—the beans you spent so much of your time and energy on earth producing!

Soft drinks of all makes and brands also abound as well as alcoholic drinks of various brands and makes—wine, beer, champagne, whisky, etc. In some cases some of the alcoholic drinks are sold at prices below that for an equal volume of water!

One does not always have to cook one's own food. One can instead visit one of the several fast food outlets or normal restaurants spread all over the country. Some of the restaurants even deliver to homes. The prices of the food served in the average restaurant are affordable to the average worker who chooses to eat there.

In short, one can usually find in an average Aburokyire setting food, food, and once more, food. Indeed, there seems to be food everywhere! You now realise how important it is for residents here to daily beseech the Lord God to lead them away from the temptation to overeat.

Failure on one's part to keep one's appetite in check can lead to various problems. Among other things, one could fall victim to one or more of the diseases that have come to be branded "civilisation diseases." The term refers to diseases that are directly or indirectly related to habits such as overeating, smoking, excess consumption of alcohol, lack of movement or exercise, etc.

18

Nowhere good!

∞

Having listened to what I have narrated in the previous chapter concerning the abundance of food in the society and its affordability to the average citizen you may be inclined to conclude that Aburokyire is inhabited by a happy and cheerful population, citizens who should be satisfied with their lives. Before I comment on that, I want to draw your attention to the Twi saying: *baabi ara nyo ye*. Others use the English term "nowhere good" to describe the same condition. Still others prefer to put it this way: "There is no heaven on earth."

That riches do not make people automatically happy and satisfied is a phenomenon observed in our society as well. How often did we hear some of the few citizens in our community everyone agreed were doing quite well in life—at least under prevailing standards—complain about this and that!

Nevertheless, I never imagined, prior to my arrival here, that anyone living in this part of the world could ever lose all hope in life and go to the lengths of committing suicide. Some may consider me naïve for harbouring these thoughts in the first place. It is true that I was quite young and inexperienced in the matters of this world prior to my arrival here. From the impression I had of the society before setting foot on Aburokyire soil, I doubt whether I would have believed anything to the contrary if I had not had the opportunity to come here and see things for myself. My attitude was based on this premise: If individuals living under the harsh conditions prevailing in our world hardly ever commit suicide, how could I expect residents living under more comfortable conditions to behave otherwise? Now I realise how wrong I was!

I didn't have to wait long after my arrival in this affluent society to learn about a case of suicide. I was at that time living in West Berlin. According to the media report, a resident of the city, a young man barely thirty years old, intentionally jumped in front of an approaching train, leading to his instant death. That tragic event occupied my mind for several days. What could have driven that individual to such a desperate act? Poverty, a job loss, a break in relations with a dear one, or what?

I reflected further on the issue, coming to the conclusion that he should have paused first to consider the conditions prevailing in many other parts of the world, such as the fate of millions of people living in abject poverty—in areas where many residents could count themselves blessed if they managed to come by a single meal each day. That thought alone might have brought the awareness home to him as to how blessed he could count himself, a thought that might have led him to reconsider his decision.

You may find it hard to swallow, but the fact is that the rate at which residents living in the Aburokyire societies commit suicide far outstrips that in an impoverished setting such as the one at our end! You may ponder over that for a while, mother!

How much do residents in the poor areas of our planet yearn for an improvement in their conditions of life! And yet those who have reached a standard of living quite beyond a level that your fantasies could ever imagine, seem, in the end, to be quite dissatisfied with their lives!

19

Christmas turned commercal

❧

Before I proceed I shall pause to pass a comment. Should someone stop a pedestrian on the streets of Mpintimpi and inquire from the individual as to the thoughts that come to his or her mind on the mention of the word "Christmas," the answer would, with all certainty, be something like: "Christmas marks the birth of Jesus Christ, whom His followers credit with being the Saviour of the world."

Should the same question be put to someone on the streets of Germany, it is likely the person would not spontaneously associate the occasion with Christ but rather reply that Christmas is a festival during which family members come together to eat good meals and exchange presents! Indeed, the religious aspect of Christmas, which is celebrated to mark the birth of a Saviour who came to lead fallen mankind back to the Creator, has almost completely been sacrificed on the alter of commerce!

At home, especially in the rural setting, only parents are expected to present their children gifts at Christmas. Strictly speaking, one cannot even describe the items involved as gifts.

Taking your children as an example, the *ntama* each of us received was needed to replace a single old piece that was getting worn out from frequent use. Wearing the same piece of cloth the whole year long usually resulted in their being worn out by the time Christmas knocked on the door. Thus the *ntama* we received on the occasion may well be regarded as an essential commodity. On the other hand, many a child living in this part of the world could well do without the presents showered on them at Christmas.

At home, children, with the exception probably of the small minority whose parents belong to the rich upper social class, are not in a position, financially, to present their parents with gifts to mark the occasion. The same is true regarding the exchange of gifts among brothers and sisters.

The picture is quite different here, where it is common practice of parents to give their children pocket money every week. From savings from such monies, many a child is able to present his or her parents, brothers and sisters, and in some cases also his or her friends gifts on the occasion.

Finding suitable gifts to present to spouses, fiancées, parents, children, brothers, sisters, not forgetting other relations such as grandpas, grandmas, cousins, etc., as well as friends close and distant, may present many a person here with a headache if not also a stomach-ache days if not weeks before the arrival of the festive day itself.

The reason does not usually lie with the issue of availability of money. No, the cause lies somewhere else, namely, the task of finding suitable gifts for loved ones, many of whom may already possess almost everything they need for this life.

The idea behind presenting others with gifts, usually, is to surprise them with items they do not possess themselves. From the background information I have provided you so far, you will agree with me that in this society the goal just referred to could be very difficult, if not impossible to achieve.

You might suggest: "If the inhabitants there have such great difficulty in the selection of gifts to please those they are intended for, why don't they renounce the practice of exchanging gifts on the occasion altogether?"

For many here that could be tantamount to doing away with Christmas altogether. Remember what I told you earlier on in regard to the spontaneous interview on the street; indeed, for many people here the word "Christmas" might as well be interchangeable with the word

"Commerce". Do away with the commercial aspect and you sweep away their main incentive for celebrating it!

You would think that after one had spent weeks pondering, considering, searching for a suitable gift to present a loved one at Christmas, and that once one finally ended up with something considered suitable, that the job would be over. That conclusion is premature, mother. As I mentioned earlier, such gifts are meant to surprise their recipients. This effect is generally considered best achieved if the gifts are first parcelled or boxed. Thus the next stage in the preparation towards gift-presentation is parcelling, or boxing.

Some supermarkets, retail shops and other shopping outlets, seek to make life a little easier for the buyer by offering free parcelling services for their customers. For the most part, however, this aspect of the procedure is shouldered by the buyer. Depending on the number of relatives, friends and associates one has, this aspect of the preparation towards Christmas might require a considerable amount of time.

In the same way that many citizens here could not imagine Christmas devoid of gifts, many could also not picture a Christmas festivity without a Christmas tree. The desire of the average citizen here to put up a Christmas tree to mark the occasion, come what may, has led to a big business developing around it.

If you happened to visit here days prior to Christmas, you would have found at various points in the city heaps of fir trees, the traditional Christmas tree, on sale. Some begin to decorate their Christmas trees days ahead of the festivities. The trees are usually placed in the living room. Others put up extra trees at the gates leading to their homes, on their balconies, in their gardens, etc.

Several days prior to Christmas day, the Christmas tree tends to become the topic of discussion for many a residents here. These could take place at home, at school, at the workplace, at various social gatherings, etc. In the process those involved are inclined not only to reveal how much money they have invested in their respective tree, but also offer the world around them an idea of the size of their tree, as well as the amount of time and energy they invested in decorating it.

"This is the most beautiful Christmas tree I have set up in years," one might be heard telling a colleague. The listener in turn might reply: "You come round and have a look at our tree; oh, it's amazing! We have decorated it with so many lights it is capable, at night, not only of illuminating the corner of the living room where it is placed but the whole room *and* our garden nearby!" There seems, indeed, to be an undeclared competition among residents here in regard not only to the size of the Christmas trees they put up, but also as to how lavishly decorated they are.

After many a resident here has succeeded in acquiring all the suitable gifts to present loved ones at Christmas and has also put up a suitable tree for the occasion, the other important issue to be considered is the appropriate food to be served on the occasion.

I have mentioned on various occasions that food abounds in this society. At every particular time one could have several types of foodstuff to select from. Much effort is invested to give the meals served at Christmas a special flavour and so make it look more special from those served on an ordinary day. In Germany a whole turkey or goose, specially roasted, is rarely absent at the dining table on Christmas day.

Beginning from about three weeks prior to the occasion, most shops in the country are packed with shop goers. A stranger to this place may well wonder if the shoppers, like hamsters, are foraging—in their case buying—in anticipation of an impending calamity or famine, as they stuff their shopping baskets and bags to the very brim with goods of all kinds. Consequently the Christmas season brings a remarkable boom in sales for shop owners here.

In Germany, Christmas is regarded purely as a family affair, a period of reunion of family members. As I told you earlier on, the word "family" has a very restrictive meaning here, standing in the main for a husband and his wife as well as their children. Many a child who has attained the age of about eighteen years moves from home to live on his or her own. The custom is for them to return home at Christmas to spend some time with their parents.

Owing to the narrow family focus that embraces the celebration of Christmas here, a stranger living here alone, far away from home, might feel even lonelier during the season. Adding to the woes of such a person is the fact that the season falls in winter, a time of year that is not only dark for a considerable period of day, but also extremely cold. The fact that much of the festivities that mark the occasion take place indoors leaves the streets very deserted. The lone stranger could thus be forced to stay at home and feel even more wretched.

Usually church attendance on an average Sunday is poor. Indeed on an average Sunday, few bother to go to Church. On such occasion, the churches are usually attended by the elderly.

The picture is totally different at Christmas. On Christmas Eve, traditionally regarded as the peak of the celebrations in Germany, most churches are completely filled with worshippers, to the extent in some cases that some attending have to stand throughout the service. Beginning from about 3 p.m. till about midnight, it is customary for churches here to hold several worship services one after the other. Attendance, in each case, is good.

This unusual phenomenon led me to ask an acquaintance of mine who would never think of visiting a normal service why he usually did so on Christmas Eve. To that he confessed that he was there not because he believed in God, but in keeping with a popular family tradition. To him going to church on Christmas may well be compared to the custom of exchanging gifts to mark the occasion.

You may want to know something about the fate of the presents their buyers took such pains to select for their beneficiaries. In Germany, such presents are usually exchanged around 8 p.m. on Christmas Eve. In the course of the day one or two members of the family gather together all the gifts family members wish to present to one another. Without usually allowing the rest of the family to get a foretaste of what awaits them, the presents are arranged beneath the Christmas tree and covered with decorating paper or cloth.

Shortly after the dinner has been enjoyed to the fullest by all, everyone gathers in the vicinity of the decorated tree. Some families may want first to sing a couple of Christmas carols to prepared their minds for the surprises awaiting them.

Finally the decisive moment arrives when the cat is let out of the bag. Usually beginning with the youngest member of the family, the presents are handed out to the beneficiaries by one member of the family. As the beneficiary whose turn it is to unravel the mystery behind the parcels goes to work to do so, the entire family looks on in tense expectation of his or her reactions.

The gifts, as I said, are meant to surprise as well as gladden the hearts of those they are intended for. On not a few occasions, though, some of them fail to achieve the desired effect; one might have ended up purchasing a dress of the wrong size; a pair of shoes meant for a dear daughter might fail to fit; a suit for the head of the family might be too loose at the waist, probably due to recent wait loss which in turn might have come as a result of the stress the person in question has been exposed to in the weeks prior to the occasion.

Even if such problems do not occur, it can happen that the beneficiary of a present already possesses the exact item, or the article in question is diametrically the opposite of the recipient's taste.

In Germany shops are closed over Christmas, and usually re-open on the 27th of December. On such days, the shops are flooded once more, this time not by shoppers rushing to purchase anything but instead by those wishing to return or exchange items which failed to please or fit them, or those they were intended for.

New Year's Eve is party time everywhere in Aburokyire! Many residents go to great lengths to organise large parties to bid farewell to the parting year and welcome in the new one. The get-togethers begin usually in the early evening and continue well into the early hours of the first day of the new year.

At midnight sirens and church bells are sounded everywhere. Then comes the moment of the fireworks! Over the next several minutes a large number of them are shot into the night air to celebrate the dawn of the new year. Admittedly, it is a beautiful scene to view, a huge number of fireworks being shot into the air to illuminate the dark midnight skies.

The big show is not without considerable costs, of course. The projection of the amount of money spent in Germany alone on such a spectacle puts the figure in several million DM. During the few days preceding New Year's Eve, it is customary in Germany for various organisations as well as some individuals of high social standing— churches, charitable organisations, leading politicians, prominent figures of society—to appeal to the general population to remember the plight of millions of poor people elsewhere in the world in need of help and to urge those wishing to spend their money on such items to donate them to charity instead.

Judging from the magnitude of the spectacle one witnesses every year, one might conclude that such appeals barely find listening ears. Apparently the majority of the human population here seems to find no suitable way to express their gratitude to Almighty God for seeing them into a new year than to help illuminate the first few minutes of the night of New Year's Day with their fireworks.

The celebrations to usher in a new year do not pass free of incidents of various dimensions, however. Not a few of them are directly or indirectly related to excessive alcohol consumption as well as incidents related to the effects of the fireworks. During the time I worked as junior doctor in various hospitals here, many a colleague detested being assigned to duty on New Year's Eve, not only because of the missed opportunity to be involved in the celebrations themselves, but also due to the expected increased workload.

Patients usually poured in shortly after midnight. They displayed injuries of various kinds—burns to the body generally caused by exploding fireworks, cuts and bruises sustained from falling as well as from fights and scuffles resulting from disputes and confrontations among friends and strangers. Much of such misunderstandings might have been over issues that under normal circumstances would not even have called for an exchange of insult.

It is customary for partygoers to consume significant quantities of alcohol in anticipation of the birth of the new year. The control over some minds ends up eventually being taken over partial or completely by "Mr/Mrs Alcohol." Little wonder that the least provocation might lead such a person to lose self-control and resort to the use of fists.

During the first week of January residents begin the task of disposing of their Christmas trees and cleaning their homes of the leaves the drying fir tree has dropped on the floors of their homes. The joy from the Christmas festivities having gone with the wind, many a person goes about this chore with reluctance.

20

"Oburoni waawu!"

❧

Before my arrival here in Germany, I used to puzzle over the term *oburoni waawu*, the name we give to the imported second-hand clothes sold on our streets at home. Let me pause to explain the term to those who are not familiar with it. The term, literally translated, means "the dead European." *Oburoni waawu*, according to the way the term is understood at home, seems to suggest clothes left over exclusively by dead—or departed—European owners.

At the time I lived in Ghana I found it difficult to believe that all the stuff being offered for sale at the stalls of the *oburoni waawu* dealers, items suitable for people of all ages and sizes, babies, little children, the youth, young adults as well as adults included, could indeed be solely the property left over by their deceased owners. Could all the heaps of second-hand children's wear, for example, have originated from dead children? Now I am better informed on the issue, mother! Strictly speaking, only a small fraction of the *oburoni waawus* on sale on our markets deserves that accolade.

A large proportion, on the other hand, might better be called *oburoni te ase* (the European still alive), for their owners, even if they happen in the meantime to be dead, surely disposed of them at a time when they were still alive. You may wish to ask: would anyone want, voluntarily, to dispose of some of the good quality clothes on sale at the stalls of the *oburoni waaawu* retailers? The answer is yes.

In a situation where the shops here are usually filled with clothes of all kinds and makes for people of all ages and sizes, the urge on many a resident here to buy some of the goods at short intervals could be too strong to resist. Some, probably out of a feeling of loneliness at home, with no one to talk to, might decide to go on a shopping spree.

Another factor that contributes to the regular changes of clothes by residents here is the weather. The two extreme weather conditions prevailing here call for the putting on of at least two sets of clothes during the year. Spring and summer usually allow for the wearing of light clothes, whereas autumn and winter generally requires one to put on thick ones.

The manufacturers of the goods already abounding in the shops as well as the agents responsible for their distribution to the consumer go to all lengths to lure the public into purchasing their products. One important means by which they seek to achieve their goal is by means of advertisements, which in some instances take a form that might well be described as aggressive.

To reach as many potential buyers as possible, including those who for one reason or another, be it laziness to walk to the shops, be it disease, be it due to lack of time, fail to frequent the shops as often as the distributors would wish them to, some shops, warehouses and other agents involved in the business of bringing products to the customer distribute catalogues portraying the articles on sale to the homes of the general population.

To enable such catalogues to achieve their desired effect—luring as many people as possible into buying the goods displayed—such catalogues display only pictures of human beings who seem to be sunning in bright side of life: good-looking and healthy babies, smiling children, young adults displaying considerable vitality, as well as adults creating the impression that all is well with them.

A glance through a typical catalogue may be enough to melt in seconds the resistance of the strong-willed person. Before such individuals realise what they are up to, they have already filled a coupon ordering several of the items on display—never mind whether they happen already to possess some of the goods ordered, or indeed whether they can afford the items.

One does not always have to make full payment for the orders from the catalogue; one is also allowed to pay by instalments. This privilege can make it even more difficult for some to resist the temptation to place an order. One could keep on ordering from the catalogue only to realise in the end how heavy the load of debt is that has accrued.

In Germany and many other countries in Aburokyire, what have come to be regarded as "sales" take place on a regular basis. During these events the prices of the goods on display are usually radically cut. It is not uncommon at such times to find goods that previously attracted a price of 100 units of currency being offered for 20 units! At such fantastic bargain prices, one might well succumb to the temptation to join the crowd in a shopping spree. In the end one could end up buying several pieces of items that may well be superfluous to one's immediate needs.

Buying, buying—and once more buying—some of the abundant goods on sale here brings with it peculiar problems of its own. The goods and clothes acquired pile up over time in the homes of their owners.

Residents here usually get round the problem by depositing clothes they wish to dispose of at special collecting points. There, special organisations and firms collect them and treat them for onward distribution to the needy of the society (yes indeed, there *is* want in this rich society as well) or for export to a developing country such as Ghana.

21

The late-night trouble-shooting of a pampered pet

&

As I mentioned earlier on, the society here is more sophisticated than the one you are used to. Partly as a result of such sophistication, many an individual resident here may resort to acts which in all certainty may appear quite strange in your ears. For example if you had the opportunity to visit me here, one of the first warnings I would give you would be as follows:

"Old lady from rural Mpintimpi, take care you do not talk loudly or cause any loud noise after 8 p.m.!"

You would probably have considered it insolent on the part of your youngest son you endured so much pain to deliver and also raise to begin to place limitations on you on the very evening of your arrival! Still, you would have been well advised to heed my advice. Should you refuse, and in the process allow your verbal protest in response to my alleged attempt to encroach on your freedom end up being too loud, that could result in the displeasure of our immediate neighbour.

That individual would probably decide to offer the villager on excursion to Aburokyire a grace period of about fifteen minutes. At the expiry of that time, should you still continue to appear loud to the person (never mind if by then you had switched to a tone which, under Mpintimpi conditions, could indeed be regarded as very quiet), she would likely ring the police to complain about the loud neighbour who was depriving her of peaceful sleep.

The law-enforcing agents would be swift to act, for German laws prohibit making disturbing noises in a residential area after 8 p.m. The officers would likely only speak a word of warning on their first appearance. If, after a while, the neighbour rang them a *second* time to complain about the noise issuing from our room, they would likely take action. The long arm of the law would have reached you on the very first day of your arrival here! The result would probably be a fine.

I shall cite two more examples to illustrate how far some residents here might go to fight for their rights. A neighbour who lived some considerable distance away from another neighbour, a dog owner, took the latter to court to demand that the court prohibit the dog from barking between certain hours of the night and the early morning. Although none of the immediate neighbours of the dog owner felt disturbed by its occasional barking during the night, the complainant who lived several metres away certainly was.

To prove her case in court she produced a large notebook to show the painstaking documentations she had made over a period of several months, recording the very minute every moment during the time period covered when she heard the dog barking!

The loud barking of the dog, she claimed, had robbed her of sleep over several months. Lack of sleep in turn had led her to suffer severe mental and emotional distress, she argued. Her argument convinced the court, which ruled to order the dog owner to either prevent her pet from barking in the night or else face a fine that amounted to a fortune.

As a final example, I shall refer to a case I read recently in the newspapers here in Hanover. The owner of a dog brought a veterinary surgeon before the court to claim a large sum of money as damages. Do you want to know the reason behind the suit?

The complainant alleged that the animal doctor had not acted timely enough to prevent the stillbirths of her dog's puppies! According to the person who brought the case, had the surgeon acted quickly enough to end the protracted labour of her dog through surgery, the six puppies would have survived. The emergency surgery he eventually conducted on the expectant mother came too late, at a time when all the little four-legged beings were already dead in the womb of their mother—or so she argued. The large sum she was demanding from the surgeon would, she said, compensate her for the severe emotional pain she suffered and continued to suffer at the time of the hearing.

Many a resident here may appreciate the argument of the dog owner or even side with her. You and I, while not denying the fact that she could have a case, may well feel dumbfounded by the ridiculous extent the woman was prepared to go as a result of the loss of the poor puppies.

Can you imagine such a situation in our setting? Never mind a dog experiencing labour difficulties—what about our human expectant mothers! At the same time the pet doctor was struggling to save the lives of the puppies, relatives of an expectant mother experiencing protracted labour in a place like Noyem, Amenamu, Adadekrom—you can list the many towns and villages surrounding us that share a common destiny with Mpintimpi—might have been struggling to find the means of transportation to bring her to hospital.

22

No privilege of permanent rest

I will dedicate this chapter to issues relating to death and burial in this society. When death happens here, relatives usually entrust the entire burial arrangements to firms known as undertakers or funeral directors. For a fee, they undertake to organise the digging of the grave, the acquisition of the coffin, the washing and dressing of the body as well as the final transport to the cemetery.

As I mentioned earlier, the strong family ties that used to prevail here in the past have broken down in a lot of places. Over here one may come across a considerable number of people, particularly the elderly, who either have no more living relations or who no longer have any contact with those still alive. Many such individuals make the necessary arrangements concerning their burial during their lifetime. They usually do so by depositing adequate sums of money at the bank to pay for the burial itself as well as the cemetery charges over a specified period of time.

What happens to people who are unable to pay for their burials themselves, and have no relatives who may do so for them? In such cases, as well as I am informed, the responsibility falls on the state to bury the dead.

The body of the deceased is usually not laid in state the way we are used to. Immediately after death, the corpse is deposited in the hospital mortuary for some time, usually a couple of days. During that period the necessary arrangements are made for the burial. On the day of burial, the coffin bearing the mortal remains is transported in a special van, usually belonging to the undertakers, to the cemetery.

Within the grounds of most graveyards here is found a church building. The coffin is first brought there for a short pre-burial ceremony. If the departed happened to be a Christian, a minister from his or her congregation officiates in a brief funeral service. This is followed by a short period during which a few selected mourners, usually close relatives, co-workers as well as other associates, deliver short farewell speeches in honour of the deceased.

In the case where the person was not a Christian or was not associated with any church, family members can hire someone specialised in such matters to give a farewell speech. Finally the coffin is wheeled to its final rest. The assembled mourners follow it on its short journey from the building to the grave.

You would not expect people who generally live isolated lives, people who had limited contacts during their lifetime, to attract a large crowd at death. That is exactly the case. Indeed, it is not uncommon to find a pastor and only a handful of mourners gathered at the cemetery to bid farewell to a departing member of the society.

At the end of a burial ceremony, the majority of mourners depart to their various homes. Usually only a handful of mourners with close ties with the family of the deceased are invited for a short reception following the burial.

The simplicity and brevity of the funeral ceremony here contrasts greatly with the extensive and time-consuming funeral rites at home.

Unlike the situation at home where the dead have the privilege of permanent rest on the piece of land on which they are buried, the dead in Germany usually have the benefit of this type of rest only for a specified period of time. Many places in Aburokyire, Germany being an example is densely populated. This has led to scarcity of land to serve as graveyards. Consequently, burial grounds are usually rented out for a specific period of time. This period varies, depending on which part of Aburokyire one lives in. My information is that in Germany this period of rest is usually between twenty-five years and thirty years. Thereafter the burial ground is allocated for another burial. My information is that the mortal remains of the previous "occupier"—only a skeleton after such a long time—is usually left undisturbed.

23

"African time"

❧

Residents here generally have a high respect for time. Anyone who arrives here from home would have to adapt quickly and learn to respect time if that person wants to adapt to the society. On the issues of work, particularly, and other official appointments, one has to take great care to keep to time. A worker who turns up late for work a couple of times risks being served a dismissal notice. Punctuality is expected not only in the official sphere but also in the private. Few people would tolerate lateness for their appointments or dates. Some might accept being up to about fifteen minutes late; lateness beyond that could evoke the indignation of many.

In this regard, residents at home have a lot to learn from their counterparts here. How much precious time is lost in our society as a result of the widespread tendency not to keep to time! In our attempt to excuse ourselves for our failings we have the tendency to refer to the so-called "African time."

Some cite the poor transportation system prevailing at home to explain why it is not always easy for residents there to keep to time. I am sceptical, however, that an improvement in our transportation system would automatically lead to punctuality on the part of many. I base this on the observations I have made regarding our nationals living in this society. When it comes to work, many of us have no choice but to go to considerable lengths to keep to time. We indeed have no alternative in this—either we adapt or risk losing our jobs. But how does the situation appear when we decide within ourselves to organise a party, a meeting, or even a church service? All of a sudden individuals who are punctual for their appointments with the native population suddenly begin to talk about "African time!"

Often events that are scheduled to begin, for example at 8 p.m., get going well after midnight! The few who choose to keep to time could find the doors to halls where the events are scheduled to take place locked and those hosting the events themselves nowhere to be found!

Should one begin to interview the late comers to find out why they could not be punctual, one is likely to hear things like: "I thought everyone else would be late so I decided to be late too!"

Should you be in a position to say a final prayer before you depart this life, please place this issue of time high on your list. Pray the Lord Almighty to send a spirit of punctuality to Africa to help boost our efforts in developing our various societies!

24

A query about the remains of African elephants

Some residents here have what I will describe as a funny idea of Africa. At the word "Africa," what comes to the mind of many a resident here ranges from a huge desert wasteland populated with a whole lot of exotic animals ranging from camels, lions, tigers, apes of various types and sizes, right down to wild snakes of all sorts.

Still others think of Africa as a huge tropical jungle boasting thick vegetation with huge trees such as mahogany, *odum*, and *owawa*, reaching at short distances from one another out of the thick canopy into the clear blue tropical skies. Populating the thick jungles is a wide range of animals— apes, gorillas, antelopes, elephants, crocodiles, huge pythons, etc.

That Africa is a vast continent composed of several different countries (albeit artificially created by the colonial masters), each in turn made up of different ethnic groups, each boasting of a language completely different from that of their next neighbour, is a fact that many a resident here is not fully aware of.

The ideas some residents here have about Africa sometime even deviate from rational thinking, as the following example illustrates. One day an argument on a matter, which in my opinion should not be a basis for argument between adults, ensued between me and a nurse here. The individual began to tease me on learning that the flesh of the antelope forms part of the meals of some communities in Africa.

"Disgusting!" he burst out. "How can anyone consume that kind of flesh?"

"Why should that upset you?" I countered. "One man's meat is another man's poison. You consume pork, others consume the flesh of the antelope, so what of it?"

No, he was not convinced. Pork was superior to the flesh of the antelope, he insisted. I did not want to prolong matters so I left things as they were. That did not mean I failed to reflect on the attitude of the staff member, nevertheless. Pork happens to be the standard meat of residents in Germany. He seemed, in effect, to want to tell me that there is no way meat eaten by the "poor African peasant" could match that of the "wealthy and enlightened" population here!

Before I leave this topic, I will narrate an experience I made as I walked on the street of Hanover. As I was rushing to catch my train for lectures, two young men approached me from the opposite direction. Just as they were about to pass me one of them stopped, took a funny look at me and shouted: "Hey boy! Where did you leave the elephants?" Just think of it, mother—they associated me with elephants just because I happen to be a person of African descent!

Whenever I tell friends and colleagues here the first time I had the opportunity to see an elephant in my life was when I visited the zoo in Berlin, some of them look at me with surprise mixed with an element of disbelief. An African travelling all the way to Europe to see an elephant for the first time is a fact, that based on their facial expression, they found hard to swallow!

25

The blessed companions of our race

∞

Residents here generally have a deep affection for pets. The love between the human owner and his or her pet can grow so strong, many owners of such animals may regard them just the way they regard their children. Indeed, to many owners of dogs or cats here these animals are so much a part of their family—just like their husbands or wives or children. For this reason many people here talk about a typical family as consisting of a couple and their two children as well as their dog or cat.

If only you had the opportunity to experience the way many an individual here treat their pets! Indeed, many a resident here allow their pets to enjoy to the full the advantages of being born into an affluent society.

In almost every supermarket one visits here, one comes across a large section offering ready-to-serve canned foodstuffs for the group of animals under discussion. Not only the basic-foodstuffs these animals need to survive are on sale in the shops; he or she who wishes to pamper his or her faithful four-legged companion with items like chocolates and other sweets specially produced for such animals can easily find a whole lot of them to buy.

We did not leave our dogs to go dirty; from time to time we took them to the riverside and gave them a wash down. The ever-present African sun helped to dry them thereafter. Places like a barber's or a beauty salon where one could send one's pet to get its hair cut and styled are beyond the thinking of citizens in a village like ours. Assuming even such shops existed in our part of the world, what proportion of pet owners there could afford to patronise them?

Not only are the above facilities available here, but one can find in some special shops cosmetics and perfumes specially manufactured to serve such animals. Some owners of cats and dogs also go to the extent of sewing suitable dresses for their friends. To make the decoration of their four-legged friends complete, some people may even put expensive jewellery on their pets!

Some owners of such animals also take pains to maintain the teeth of their pets. They regularly brush the teeth of their pets with appropriate toothbrushes and toothpastes.

When, in spite of such preventive measures, problems develop with the teeth of their pets, they can take them to dentists who have specialised in that, too. I recently saw in a leading German magazine a picture showing a cat whose two problem teeth had been replaced by two artificial ones made of gold! That indeed is the extent to which some people here may go to show their love and affection for their pets!

In case of sickness, one can take his or her sick pet to one of the many veterinary clinics. If you had had the opportunity to visit me here, I would have taken you to the reception of a veterinary clinic to see things for yourself! You would have had the opportunity to experience at first hand the wonderful love some owners of dogs and cats have for their pets.

Whilst we mingled with the considerably large number of people waiting patiently at the reception for their turn to bring their sick pets to the doctor, somebody might rush in from outside cuddling a sick dog and with bubbling hysteria begin to cry: "Where is the doctor? Please, please allow me to see the doctor immediately; my darling is dying! Please have mercy on me!"

If the doctor by chance comes out of the consulting room to pick up something from the reception area, the following conversation could ensue between the physician and the emotional newcomer:

"Please doctor, have mercy on my beloved dog! Please save my darling from dying. Do everything you can to help it. It is my only companion. It is a dear and faithful friend. My God, how can I exist without it?!"

"Be calm, good lady," the veterinary doctor might reply. "We will do our best to help."

"Do you think this sweet little dog is going to die, doctor?"

"I cannot say anything at the moment. I have to examine it first."

"Oh my God, have mercy on Efi. Please be merciful to my precious dog. I cannot live without it. If it dies, I will die with it!"

After examining the dying dog, the doctor might decide on surgery.

"The little dog needs an urgent operation!"

"What are the chances?"

"50-50."

"Please be fast, Doc. Save that dog."

"The surgery will cost about 1000 DM!"

"Do not think about money! What is money to me? Doesn't my name tell you everything? I am the owner of the supermarket chain bearing the same name. You just save my dog and you will not regret you did it."

You might assume that the love the dog-owner had for the pet would end should the poor creature fail to survive the proposed surgery! That usually is not the case. Indeed, many a pet owner here invest their time and money to give their dead pets a fitting burial! There are found in many areas in Aburokyire special cemeteries where pets like cats and dogs are buried. Special firms that organise the burial of such animals for a fee are found here.

In some extreme cases, some pet owners go to the extent of hiring special horse-drawn wagons to transport the boxes containing the remains of their pets to the pet cemetery, a measure that might cost a considerable amount of money.

Just as it is customary here for people to pay regular visits to the graves of their dead human relatives, so too do a lot of pet owners pay regular visits to the graves. On such occasions some of them lay bouquets of flowers on the graves, just as they would do for their dead human relatives!

26

A free ride on the German highway

❧

The countries in the West are classified as developed, whereas the countries in Africa are generally described as developing or even underdeveloped. Personally, I am not happy with the tendency of human beings to subdivide or subclassify our common planet into groups, associations and what have you.

Still in looking at the standard of development of the infrastructure here, vis-à-vis that standard pertaining in a place like Ghana, one cannot help but admit the fact that indeed there is a remarkable gap between the level of the infrastructural development in Germany and other western industrialised countries as compared to the situation prevailing in Ghana and other countries in the developing world. I will now proceed to provide you a brief overview of the infrastructural development in Germany.

Germany boasts a highly-developed road network. Almost every town or village in Germany, no matter the size, is linked with a tarred road. One hardly comes across a pothole on the roads here. The major towns and cities are connected to one another by way of broad and modern highways. Some such highways have as many as three lanes leading in the same direction. At short distances along the highways are filling stations, restaurants, motels, telephones as well as police stations. Most of these facilities operate around the clock.

Almost every adult here possesses a driving licence. The minimum age required to drive in several countries in Aburokyire is 18 years. In some such countries one may even acquire such a permit at the age of 16 years. Many persons acquire the permission to drive not just for the sake of possessing one but also because they also acquire their own car not long afterwards. Indeed, the great majority of able-bodied adults here possess their own cars.

27

A train ride deep under the ocean floor

⚭

An extensive railway network exist in several countries in Aburokyire, Germany being no exception. The trains are fast and modern. Towns and villages not directly linked by rail are connected to the nearest available train station by bus.

Apart from trains linking towns and cities together, there are also special electric trains that operate within the cities and big towns themselves. They have their stations scattered at several places in such areas where they stop at short and regular intervals to serve travellers. Those parts of town that are not directly linked by rail are served by buses. The public transportation system in most towns and cities are so reliable one could well do without one's own private car.

At this stage, I want you to pay extra attention to what you are about to hear. Some of the trains serving the cities travel on the surface of the earth. Inner-city railways are not restricted to the surface of the earth, however, for some also travel beneath the earth's surface.

"Trains travelling beneath the surface of the earth!" I hear you exclaim. "Do you expect me to believe such a fairy tale?"

Well, take it from me, mother, that is the truth and nothing but the truth!

With this revelation, no doubt, it will probably have dawned on you just how different the world you spent your life in is in comparison to the one here. When I first heard about the underground trains I, too, could not imagine how the system functions until I arrived here to see things for myself. Take it from me—it is an astounding feat of human engineering ingenuity.

The constructors dug deep beneath the surface of the earth to build suitable tunnels through which trains are capable of travelling. You might think the system is made up of only one rail track that enables the trains to travel in one direction at a time. No, that is not the case. The system has been built to permit in several instances more than one train using it simultaneously, and travelling in both directions.

At certain points, the underground tunnels widen to allow for rail junctions, or intersections, as well as branches. In some large cities a single underground rail track could cover a distance of fifty kilometres and beyond in one direction.

At several points on the underground rail system, stations have been constructed to enable passengers to get on board or leave the trains. Such stations, some of which are located several metres under the earth's surface, are reached with the help of steps, lifts or escalators.

Escalators and lifts! How do I describe them to your understanding? They are machines constructed to convey people and goods from a higher to a lower level and vice versa. It is especially helpful for travellers with children, the old as well as the handicapped.

The underground network may well pass under a busy city centre, just beneath an area where tall and mighty buildings are located. Some such buildings are so tall one has to strain ones eyes to get a glimpse of their tops.

"Such huge buildings can stand above the underground tunnels without collapsing into them?" you may ask. That, indeed, is the case. The underground—it is a fascinating masterpiece of human technology.

Elsewhere in Aburokyire, engineers have even managed to dig a tunnel deep under the seabed to create a link between mainland Europe and a nearby island, the UK. The Eurotunnel, as it is called, has facilitated a direct rail link—direct "land" traffic as it were—between mainland Europe and the British Isles separated by about 60 kilometres of ocean water.

28

Hotels floating on the wide, wide ocean

∞

Did you ever get the opportunity to visit the harbour at Tema during one of your visits to Osei? If you did, you probably would have seen a ship close at hand. Ships are usually mighty objects built to travel on the surface of the sea. Some are as large as a mighty building. That such huge objects are capable of floating is indeed astounding. Just think of an ordinary stone; the moment one throws it into water it sinks! A large object like a ship, on the other hand, though it is in the main constructed from metal or iron, which is heavier than water, has the ability to float! The details as to how this is made possible will not interest you at this stage of your life, I guess.

During my early years as a student of the Hanover Medical School, a trip was organised for the foreign students to an island about an hour's ride from the northern tip of Germany. That was my first opportunity to travel on a ship. A journey on a ship could present the traveller, especially the first traveller, with considerable difficulty. With the world around seeming to tilt or rotate before one's own eyes, one can get dizzy. That might result in a feeling of nausea that eventually can lead to vomiting. To avoid or at least to minimise the impact of such symptoms, generally referred to as seasickness, travellers may have to take suitable medication minutes before they begin their journeys.

One might well describe some of these ships as floating hotels. On board some of them are facilities that seem to promise some touch of heaven to many a wearied inhabitant of our trouble-infested world—

sleeping rooms (called cabins) decorated with all the expensive furniture one could imagine, restaurants serving some of the best dishes available on earth, swimming pools boasting the best setting, etc. Residents here who can afford it pay large sums of money to spend some weeks and in some cases months on such luxury liners.

29

A man-made "bird" battling with tons of cargo

❧

I consider it inappropriate to conclude this chapter on transportation without devoting some time to air transport. At the end of all my visits to Ghana you came to the airport to see me off. These visits gave you the opportunity to see some of the planes on the tarmac, even if at considerable distance.

At home we have a couple of airports. Needless to say, in Germany one comes across several large airports—not only in the major cities, but also in several large towns. Several airlines regularly frequent the various airports.

The aeroplane, it is generally accepted, represents one of the greatest inventions of mankind. Without it, the idea would probably never have occurred to me to venture on a journey to a place several thousand kilometres from our little village! How much I wished that you would also get the opportunity to travel on an airplane in your lifetime!

The aircraft you saw me board at the airport in Accra—when you saw me off on my last visit—is capable of carrying over three hundred passengers! I have not even included the several kilograms of accompanying cargo!

"How is an aeroplane laden with such a heavy burden able to lift up from the ground to fly in the air?" you may ask That is a question the experts of aviation can satisfactorily answer! Layman as I am, I can only tell you, on the basis of my elementary physics, that an aircraft is endowed with very powerful engines capable of generating sufficient energy and speed at take off to enable the huge colossus to overcome the forces of gravity and lift into the air.

Forces of gravity! How do I expect you to understand a concept like that! I will try to explain. When a stone is thrown into the air, it travels up to a certain height only to fall back to the ground after a while. This is because a force acts on it to pull it back towards the earth. This force is what is known as "the force of gravity."

For the plane to be able to move into the air and stay there it needs to overcome this force. After it has successfully taken off, it climbs to a great height above the clouds. After attaining a suitable height defined by the pilot, it is normally kept there throughout the flight.

"How is it able to keep its course in the sky?" you may ask. Aircraft are equipped with complicated instruments that point the pilots to their desired destinations.

When the man-made bird is about to reach its destination, the pilot initiates appropriate steps to ensure a successful landing. Returning the aeroplane, which has been flying at a considerable speed over high altitudes, back to earth, is a feat of its own. First, the pilot brings about a gradual reduction in flight altitude.

After an appropriate descent has been achieved, the final touchdown manoeuvre is begun. Passengers are at that stage called upon to fasten their seat belts. Still moving at considerable speed, the aircraft makes a sloping descent towards the airport. The aircraft is usually filled with silence as the passengers go through some of the decisive moments of the flight.

In a manner akin to a flying bird about to make a landing on the ground, lowering its feet to support the landing, the wheels of the plane are lowered from the belly of the plane just before it touches down on earth.

At touchdown there is rumbling and shaking of the whole aircraft. The aeroplane is allowed to roll a distance along the tarmac to bring about a gradual reduction in speed. Eventually the man-made flying object comes to a complete stop; passengers may then disembark.

One may rightly describe the aeroplane as an artificial bird flying at high velocities high up in the skies. It is, for example, capable of travelling the considerable distance between Ghana and Germany in a matter of about seven hours. A fast-moving car, on the other hand, would take days if not weeks to accomplish that.

If one happens to fly on a sunny day, one may get the opportunity to observe the clouds, the seas, the fields, the mountains, etc., from the windows. In the face of the vastness of creation unfolding before one's own eyes, one appears minute and insignificant in one's own eyes.

The invention of the aeroplane, indeed, represents a significant milestone in man's technological advancement.

30

Monitoring patients sky-high

T he medical system in Aburokyire, Germany being a typical example, is very advanced indeed. Human beings resident here profit from the existing impressive medical infrastructure.

If a farmer here were to have an accident on his or her farm, all that that person need do would be to get hold of his or her cell phone and dial the emergency services. If the farm happened to be inaccessible by road, the emergency service would alert the medical emergency helicopter also known as the air ambulance.

Such a helicopter is supplied with all the necessary medical equipment as well as medication needed to treat a seriously ill patient. Within minutes it would be in the air. A doctor and at least one medical assistant would accompany the pilot. After they had administered the basic first aid needed to stabilize the patient's condition, they would fly him or her to the nearest hospital suited to handle the condition.

During the flight, the medical personnel would continuously carry out what the experts refer to as "monitoring." That is, they would regularly check the patient's blood pressure, heartbeat, breathing, state of awareness, etc.

By means of modern communication equipment, the doctor would communicate with the hospital they were flying to, to inform them about the patient's current condition and advise them on the necessary preparations they needed to make to ensure a smooth transfer of the patient from the helicopter to the hospital.

If, in the opinion of the doctor accompanying the patient, an emergency operation were necessary, he would advise the stand-by operation team on the preparations needed to be done. By the time of landing, a team of doctors, nurses and other personnel would be fully prepared to continue with the measures already begun.

When emergencies occur at one's home, one can also count on doctors who will arrive in no time to offer their services. Depending on the case involved, the doctor may decide to treat the patient on the spot or call the ambulance to take the sick person to a suitable hospital. At any time of the day, irrespective of which part of the country one finds oneself in, one can be sure of prompt medical attention in the case of medical emergency.

In normal day-to-day life, when one falls sick, the first person one contacts is one's family doctor. Their practices are spread throughout the country. One usually does not have to travel far to reach the next available family doctor. Depending on one's complaint, the GP (General Practitioner), or family doctor, may decide to treat one personally or refer one to a specialist who could also be just around the corner.

If, in the opinion of the general practitioner, a patient's case requires treatment in hospital, the family doctor initiates steps to get the sick person to a suitable hospital. Hospitals abound in Germany; one usually has to travel only a short distance to reach the nearest one.

31

"Home, sweet home!"

⁂

Before I finally drop my pen, I will briefly shed some light on the lot of the Ghanaian community in Germany in particular and Aburokyire in general. As I mentioned at the beginning of this discourse, there is an exaggerated expectations concerning the situation prevailing in Aburokyire. After staying here over ten years I have come to agree with the saying "home, sweet home."

You also remember the Twi saying, *"wo nsa akyiri be ye wo de a ente se wo nsa yem"* (No matter how delicious the back of your hand tastes, it can never taste better than your palm.) It is true that the standard of living in Aburokyire far outmatches that of Ghana, No matter how comfortable the living conditions here are, there is a permanent longing in my heart for home. Based on the conversation I have had with many of our nationals here I am led to believe that the situation is not different with the majority of them.

In my opinion, the real way forward is for Ghana, Africa and the rest of the developing world to make strenuous efforts to develop their respective countries, to guarantee a certain living standard—not the same standard achieved in the West, but a standard of living that ensures adequate daily meals, decent accommodation, basic health and the availability of a respectable infrastructure.

It is a goal not unattainable. Yes indeed, if African leaders could be selfless and dedicated to the good of all, instead of fanning their own selfish interests and greed—greed that leads some to loot the national coffers empty—we could attain a decent standard of living that could make travelling elsewhere in search of greener pastures unattractive.

That is not to say that I am advocating a complete ban on our citizens travelling to the West. On the streets of several European countries one usually sees visitors from Japan. They usually travel to the West as tourists, stay for a while and return to their country. In the same way, some residents here visit us a tourists.

If we developed our own countries to make us feel comfortable at home, we could then, like tourists from Japan, South Korea, Singapore etc, visit here, book ourselves into hotels, sightsee for a time, then return to our various countries.

That is the challenge for our political leaders. Yes Africa needs honest, selfless and dedicated politicians, leaders who will guarantee good governance, a prerequisite for sustained economic development. If indeed you have the energy to say a last prayer before you depart this world, then please plead with Almighty God to send good governance to Ghana in particular and Africa in general. In the meantime, however, I will narrate briefly the lot of fellow Ghanaians here, to let you know in particular what we do for a living.

You might still remember the Twi saying, *"ohwoho na edi abebe sere."*

For those not conversant with our language it means something like: it is the stranger who is served a cockroach leg.

Towards the end of the 1970s and the beginning of the 1980s several thousand Ghanaians left the country for Nigeria in search of greener pastures. Thanks to the global oil crisis of the period, the economy of the oil rich country was booming offering the new arrivals jobs and other opportunities to earn money.

Eventually I joined the bandwagon and headed for "Agege," the term that we in Ghana used to refer to our oil rich neighbour. When we got there, we craved jobs that the natives were reluctant to perform themselves—working on construction sites, as labourers on farms, as factory hands etc.

If we had to perform the dirty work in another African country, you can imagine the situation would not be any different in Aburokyire.

Aburokyire indeed is a sophisticated society. Most of the countries here, Germany being a typical example, have their own citizens who are highly trained in various fields of human endeavour—doctors, engineers, lawyers, accountants and what have you.

On the other hand the great majority of citizens of our country who made it here through the political asylum process I explained earlier, are uneducated or at best semi-educated. That is not to say that there are no highly-educated and skilled Ghanaians in Aburokyire. Of course there are. Many of the individuals in that category came here to study and for various reasons stayed on after their studies. They form a small minority of the Ghanaian population however.

What type of work do you expect a mostly untrained work force to find in this highly sophisticated society? When they manage to acquire working permits (acquiring such permits here can be a tug of war; I want to spare you the details however), many eventually end up as cleaners, dish washers, factory hands, farm assistants hands helping to harvest tomatoes, apples, cabbage etc.

Prior to my admission to medical school, at the time when I lived as an asylum seeker in Berlin, I also worked occasionally as a cleaner in the homes of some members of our church I attended.

As a student, one is usually allowed to work during the holidays, though some countries place restrictions on the number of hours one is allowed to work per week. As a student one could find work as a factory hand, as a helping hand at a fast food restaurant, as sales assistant at a grocery shop, a security officer in a shop etc. In my case, by virtue of being a medical student, I found work as a ward assistant in various hospitals.

Life here is far from easy, yes far from what we picture at home. The personal experience I had when I set foot on the soil of Germany may be considered as typical. First came the euphoria and the excitement then the sobriety as the hard realities of life here began to unfold before my eyes. In due course it dawned on me that Aburokyire after all is not the paradise I had imagined back home.

It is true that goods abound in the shops, the means to acquire them is not easy to come by however. Yes indeed one has to work hard to make ends meet in this society.

Even when one is desirous and capable of working, one's immigration status could stand in one's way. Without a residence permit one is denied a working permit. Without a work permit hardly any employer will risk employing one for fear of coming into conflict with the law, a situation that could lead to the imposition of a heavy fine, if not imprisonment. Without work to earn the needed income, one can only window shop from one shop to other. With the abundance of goods staring one in the face, one can be led into various temptations.

What I have just touched upon can end in disillusionment, frustration, depression and what have you. I have on several occasions come across our nationals who have regretted their decision to travel to Europe. Some of them were running businesses back home, businesses that were doing well. The hope of greener pastures in the West led them to sell such businesses, only to end up in stranded in Europe—without proper immigration papers, without jobs and in some cases without even a place to lay their heads. Some would be delighted to board the next available plane bound for Accra, if only they had the means to purchase the needed ticket!!

32

Farewell kind-hearted, bold and outspoken old woman!

I have at last come to the end of my letter. It is my hope that it is read to you before you depart this life. Even more important—it is my hope that you do not succumb to death so soon as to prevent me from meeting you to bid you a personal farewell. Mortals that you and I are, we have no absolute control over tomorrow. I have therefore written this piece as if it were my last words to you before your departure. Yours has been a life of goodness, love, hard work and sacrifice. You have cause to congratulate yourself for what you achieved in lif

That a poor, illiterate woman, born into one of the poorest surroundings one could find in our troubled world, was able to raise a child who could end up as a medical doctor in one of the richest countries on earth, is something you can surely be proud of. Not that I want in any way to blow our trumpets before the whole world. Boasting, after all, was not part of your nature. I have indeed sought all along to emulate that virtue of yours.

Before I finally drop my pen, I want to raise an issue over which you might reflect upon in your final moments on earth. Supposing you were given the chance to enter the world a second time and that this time round you were given the choice to decide on matters like the sex and skin colour you would be endowed with as well as the social status of the parents you would be born to, would you come back the way you did on the first occasion—female and black? Moreover, would you agree once again to be born into Amantia, the little town on the edge of the equator, part of an impoverished continent struggling desperately to free itself from the tentacles of bitter poverty?

Fare thee well, kind-hearted, brave and courageous woman!

33

EPILOGUE: An invitation from beyond

࿇

I started writing the original edition of the this book in the middle of 1994 and completed the job in about nine months. The abridged edition which you have just gone through was completed in October 2011.

Much has happened in our troubled world since then. Worthy of mention, as far as the issues I touched upon in my last communication with my dying mother is concerned, is the fact that the Euro has replaced the Deutsche Mark (DM) as the national currency of Germany.

At present there is much moaning going on in the countries which use the Euro official currency concerning the debt problems of some of the countries in the "Euro Club" and the potential threat such debts pose to the stability of the common European currency.

As regards the situation of residents in the little village Mpintimpi where my late mother spent the greater part of her earthly life, I can report that there has been some improvement in their living conditions as compared to the situation that persisted there during her life time.

In particular, the village has benefited from the national electrification programme began in Ghana in early the 1990s and which has the goal of providing electricity to as many places in the country as possible. The village profited from the fact that the electric power lines constructed to link two major towns passed along the fringes of the village. Eventually an extension was made to the village, permitting those who could afford it to be supplied with electricity. Nevertheless, though electricity is available in theory, only a small fraction of residents can afford it, forcing the majority to rely on kerosene lamps.

Concerning the supply of water, there is still no piped water in the village. The village in the meantime however has benefited from a well-drilling programme of the Government. The village has a few wells, operated with hand pumping machines. The quality of the water is generally said to be good.

Also thanks to the advent of the mobile phone, I am now able to communicate directly with my relatives there from far away Europe, a situation that would certainly have fascinated my late mother.

Despite the aforesaid, it is nevertheless basically true to say that the standard of living of residents of Mpintimpi vis-à-vis those of residents in Hanover in the year 2011 has remained still very wide apart, today, just as it was the case when mother parted this life in 1994.

The challenge of the future is for strenuous efforts to be undertaken by world leaders, wherever they are from, to improve the living standards of the rural population of our planet, wherever they happen to be.

Mother, in typical fashion, would today, just as she would have done during her life time if she had had the opportunity to visit rich West, certainly want to extend this invitation to her compatriots now moaning in the West as a result of a perceived fall in their standard of living:

"Hello, fellow residents of planet earth living at the bright side of our troubled planet! You who are fighting in vain to shed superfluous weight! All you need do is to purchase a plane ticket and come over to spend some time with us here at Mpintimpi. You need not trouble yourself with thoughts of where you will stay or what you will eat. We will provide that for free. Oh yes, I can assure you, you can count on our hospitality! Do not expect any preferential treatment, though, when you get here. Instead, you will be served the same type and quantity of food as anyone else in the village; you will walk the same distance like anyone else to help us work on our fields; you will also assist us to carry on our daily household chores—sweep the compound with brooms, travel considerable distances to fetch water from the stream, help pound fufu, help in dish washing, etc. Take it from me: after spending some weeks with us, under the conditions prevailing in our little village, you are guaranteed a hundred percent success at weight loss—not only during your stay, but with all certainty ever after! Why am I so sure of that? Indeed, the thought of your dear friends in our little village struggling each day to find food will help you each day to resist the temptation to eat too much!"

Robert Peprah-Gyamfi
Loughborough UK,
October 2011

www.ingramcontent.com/pod-product-compliance
Lightning Source LLC
Chambersburg PA
CBHW022304060426
42446CB00007BA/586